THE GIANT'S LADDER

THE GIANT'S LADDER

THE SCIENCE PROFESSIONAL'S BLUEPRINT

FOR MARKETING SUCCESS

ELIZABETH CHABE

Advantage | Books

Published by Advantage Books, Charleston, South Carolina.
An imprint of Advantage Media.

ADVANTAGE is a registered trademark, and the Advantage colophon is a trademark of Advantage Media Group, Inc.

Printed in the United States of America.

10 9 8 7 6 5 4 3 2 1

ISBN: 978-1-64225-602-4 (Paperback)
ISBN: 978-1-64225-601-7 (eBook)

Library of Congress Control Number: 2023920522

Cover design by Megan Elger.
Layout design by Matthew Morse.

To my mom.

CONTENTS

ABOUT THE AUTHOR

ELIZABETH CHABE (MBA, MS) is an author, entrepreneur, and recognized strategic marketing consultant for science, engineering, and technology organizations. Her work has been featured in the *New York Times*, *Entrepreneur*, CNBC, Composites World, and 360Dx, among others.

As the founder and CEO of High Touch Group, Elizabeth oversees a team that develops marketing and PR strategies for advanced science, engineering, and technology organizations. Through High Touch Group's holistic, comprehensive marketing services, clients generate more leads, drive revenue, and elevate their brands into the global B2B space. Her work as a strategic consultant has been instrumental to biotechnology, energy, advanced materials, advanced manufacturing, and robotics and automation companies.

Since her first business venture at the age of nine, Elizabeth has built and overseen countless successful research programs and marketing teams. As the former senior manager of digital and strategic marketing at the Jackson Laboratory (JAX), she developed the marketing strategies for its mouse model portfolio, model generation (CRISPR), and in vivo contract research services. Prior to joining JAX, she oversaw global communications for the Advanced Structures and Composites Center in Maine. There, she managed projects including the center's offshore wind research program, the largest research and R&D program in Maine's history.

Since 2018, Elizabeth has been a governor-appointed director of the Maine Venture Fund.

An inveterate traveler, she splits her time between the US and developing world communities. She currently resides in Mexico with her husband and rescue dogs.

ACKNOWLEDGMENTS

Writing acknowledgments is a tricky process. On the one hand, there are so many people who have contributed to this book and my career who I would like to recognize. On the other hand, doing so might take more pages than the book itself.

I'd be remiss if I didn't first acknowledge the staff at the University of Maine's Advanced Structures and Composites Center for offering such a fertile training ground. Habib, Jake, Doreen, Bob, Larry, and the rest of the team: it is with your unparalleled support and guidance that I built my first science marketing team. You have made a difference in so many young professionals' lives. You certainly did in mine.

I'm thankful for my clients who, over the years, have helped me and my team hone our process. Many of them were early readers of this text, and their feedback was immensely helpful.

I'd also like to acknowledge my incredible team—past, present, and future. Your collective insights, relentless dedication, and unyielding support have not only shaped our success but have also created a culture of collaboration and excellence that propels us forward. Your contributions are the backbone of our achievements, and I am deeply grateful for the opportunity to work alongside such talented individuals.

Thank you to my husband for being my editor-in-chief. This book would not exist without you. Also thank you to my siblings who, even though we all live very far apart, supported me through this entire project.

Thank you to the many friends and colleagues who became editors, researchers, sounding boards, or providers of other support. You have my gratitude. A special thank you to Sam, Dimitri, and John. Your careful feedback made all the difference.

TAKING THE FIRST STEP

Using a metaphor coined generations earlier, Isaac Newton once wrote, "If I have seen further, it is by standing on the shoulders of giants." In context, Newton's "giants" represent the brilliant minds who forever altered our understanding of and interaction with the world. Their discoveries unlocked new realms of possibility once unimaginable. Their "shoulders," then, provide the foundations that countless subsequent researchers have used to progress their own work. Scientific progress is fundamentally reliant on past discoveries, which pave the way for further exploration and understanding.

My intention is not to bore you with an idea easily found in memes, valedictorian speeches, or the titles of rock albums (it's true). Rather, it's to remind you of a simple truth: that none of us—not you, not me, not Elon Musk, nor the US surgeon general—start from scratch. No one goes it alone. We all stand on the shoulders of giants in one way or another—through scholarship, mentorship, network effects, inheritances, and more.

From a scientific perspective, Newton's own field is one of the best examples of this concept. Our understanding of the universe began with classical physics, pioneered by the likes of Galileo Galilei and Johannes Kepler. When Newton stepped in, he created a unified framework that defined the laws of motion and universal gravitation (*Philosophiae Naturalis Principia Mathematica*, 1687).

WE ALL STAND ON THE SHOULDERS OF GIANTS IN ONE WAY OR ANOTHER.

However, his work—absolutely groundbreaking at the time—was not the culmination but rather the foundation of modern physics.

Just over two centuries later, another giant appeared on the scene: Albert Einstein. Using Newtonian physics as his foundation, Einstein proposed the theory of special relativity, which revolutionized our understanding of space and time (*On the Electrodynamics of Moving Bodies*, 1905). This shift in perception led to the broader theory of general relativity, which describes gravity as a curvature of space-time (*The Foundation of the General Theory of Relativity*, 1916). Einstein's theories, in turn, became the stepping stone for the development of quantum mechanics, an area of physics that addresses phenomena at the atomic and subatomic levels.

These advances in physics have given rise to quantum computing, a field built on the principles of quantum mechanics. Traditional computers use bits that can be in a state of either zero or one. Quantum computers, however, utilize quantum bits (or "qubits"), which, due to superposition and entanglement, can exist in multiple states simultaneously and can even be connected across space.

The implications of this are tremendous. The hypothetical computational power of a quantum computer significantly outstrips that of the most powerful classical supercomputers. This could revolutionize just about everything, from cryptography to drug discovery, climate modeling, space travel, and materials science.

Today, as researchers around the world work to overcome the technological challenges of building scalable, reliable quantum computers, they are each making their own contributions to this chain of knowledge. Each discovery is a step forward that will be built upon by the researchers who come after them.

In our fast-paced, hyperconnected world, scientific knowledge is no longer a static entity stuck within the confines of a library. Instead, it's more like light—both focused and expansive, rapidly traveling across the digital universe, illuminating worlds, and allowing us to see more clearly. Innovations no longer require a physical space to be shared or discussed. Platforms such as ResearchGate, arXiv and bioRxiv, Reddit, and GitHub have transformed into the new "libraries," open, accessible, and brimming with information—and are then amplified by social media, podcasts, conferences, and traditional media. Groundbreaking scientific dialogues now echo across these digital platforms, accessible to anyone, anywhere.

Isn't this remarkable? We're witnessing the tipping point of the age-old process of scientific iteration across multiple fields as a public. One could argue that Newton's metaphor of "standing on the shoulders of giants" has found a new interpretation in the form of our globally intertwined digital network and the marketing—yes, marketing!—infrastructure that supports it.

WAIT ... MARKETING?

Science is a realm of giants—thinkers and innovators whose groundbreaking work lights the path for those who follow. Yet, in the contemporary landscape, the scope of their responsibilities often extends far beyond making groundbreaking discoveries and sharing their work within the academic bubble of peer-reviewed journals and conferences.

Today's scientist must expertly navigate online platforms such as ResearchGate, sharing their work not just with colleagues but also with a globally distributed audience. They must be prepared to articulate complex ideas in simplified, relatable terms on popular podcasts, becoming an emissary of their discipline to the public and other experts alike.

And for those who harbor an entrepreneurial spirit, there's a further expansion of their job description. They find themselves pitching to investors, showcasing their work's commercial potential, and demonstrating progress—or what's referred to in business parlance as "traction." They are tasked with translating the theoretical into the tangible, converting abstract ideas into marketable products. This metamorphosis has gradually redefined the scientist's traditional role, integrating elements that were once alien to their domain—selling, raising capital, and marketing.

In fact, the last decade has seen a significant increase in the number of science-driven entrepreneurial ventures and university spinouts with scientists at the helm who have been a driving force in this rise. Between 2013 and 2022, equity funding for university spinouts globally totaled more than $158 billion and at a hockey stick–shaped pace, according to a report from Global University Venturing.[1] This growth is indicative of a broader trend where scientific innovation is increasingly driving new business opportunities.

While the discipline of science communications emphasizes sharing and disseminating scientific knowledge—the important job

---

1   Thierry Heles, "University spinouts double fundraising in the last decade," Global University Venturing, January 2023, accessed September 26, 2023, https://global-venturing.com/university/spinouts-double-fundraising-in-ten-years/.

of *educating*—these emerging roles go a step further. They require scientists to not only educate but also *persuade*, transforming their potential audience into clients, customers, or investors. Data dissemination isn't enough to persuade. You must learn to generate interest, spark desire, and drive action.

In essence, this evolution in roles has given birth to a new domain—science marketing. This field operates at the intersection of science, business, and communication, blending elements from each to create a unique, multifaceted discipline. This evolving dynamic provides an exciting and challenging opportunity for scientists— serving as the vanguards of their field, they also have the potential to become its ambassadors and entrepreneurs.

Marketing—a profession fueled by human psychology and analytics—might seem distasteful or alien to scientists who are more at home with p-values, control groups, and reproducible results. Unfortunately, even the most impactful scientific advancements and their applications may be overlooked due to ineffective communication, insufficient exposure, and a persistent belief in the outdated notion of "if we make a significant discovery, recognition will follow."

THE EXPOSURE CONUNDRUM

Every path to discovery is marked by a common foe: the exposure conundrum. It's a struggle between two oftentimes diametrically opposed pursuits: the toil of creation and the challenge of gaining recognition. You worked hard for that discovery or to develop that product—so why isn't your hard work paying off? Unfortunately, many scientists are familiar with the bitter taste of obscurity despite their commitment to their craft.

The scientist's journey comprises long hours, meticulous efforts, and the relentless pursuit of something novel. This is the way we're told it works: we begin the chosen path with rigorous training and education, and all of that culminates in esteemed positions in academia and research institutions. But too often the shared enemy—the exposure conundrum—manifests itself. The scientist, despite their best efforts, grapples with bringing their work to the attention of a wider audience.

Navigating this challenge is no trivial task. The worlds of academia and industry present formidable challenges. The scientist must navigate the winding roads of funding, research publishing, and technology commercialization. Increasingly often, they need to identify potential uses of their technology, understand its applications, and devise strategies to reach these people and pique their interest. The essence of the exposure conundrum lies in this struggle—you've achieved a breakthrough or innovation, yet the challenge remains in gaining the visibility and recognition it deserves.

In the modern era of rapid data flows, the exposure conundrum becomes even more prominent. The complex, nuanced work of scientists competes with an ever-growing array of distractions. To make a difference, dedicated individuals must not only advance their fields but also make their findings accessible and engaging to various audiences, from journalists and funders to businesses, customers, and government agencies.

This challenge presents scientists with a twofold problem:

1. How to distill the essence of their work into narratives that resonate with those outside their fields
2. How to communicate those narratives in captivating and inspiring ways

Failure to do so can confine even the most brilliant minds to obscurity, their work hidden from the world. You may have even experienced this yourself: a breakthrough in your lab that barely makes a ripple outside it.

Consider the work of Dr. Herbert Boyer and Dr. Stanley Cohen in the early 1970s, which laid the foundation for modern genetic engineering. These scientists successfully developed the first method for combining and replicating genes from different species, a breakthrough that would revolutionize the field of biotechnology.

Despite the immense potential of their discovery, Boyer and Cohen's work initially struggled to gain traction outside of specialized academic circles. The revolutionary nature of their research, coupled with the lack of immediate commercial applications, led to a lag in widespread recognition and funding.

However, this situation changed dramatically when Boyer cofounded Genentech, one of the first biotechnology companies. By connecting scientific innovation with entrepreneurial acumen, Boyer and his colleagues were able to translate a laboratory discovery into tangible products, including vital medicines such as recombinant insulin.

The journey from groundbreaking research to commercial success was fraught with challenges, including the struggle to communicate the value and potential of genetic engineering to investors, regulators, and the public. Boyer and Cohen's story underscores the delicate balance between discovery and exposure, illustrating how even transformative innovations can remain hidden in the shadows without effective communication and marketing strategies—another victim of the exposure conundrum.

MARKETING FOR SCIENCE (IT'S NOT ALL EASY)

I offer you a solution to the exposure conundrum: the marketing-savvy scientist. Sounds unconventional, right? Yet this might be the key to overcoming obscurity in science. Just as a riveting performance can captivate a crowd, effective science marketing has the power to cut through noise and connect creators with an audience. Fine-tuned messaging can amplify a scientist's work and transform ideas into lasting legacies. But let's be clear: it's not all smooth sailing.

Consider a purely hypothetical scientist named Kiran, a microbiologist dedicated to unlocking the secrets of antibiotic resistance. Kiran's journey was punctuated by accolades, publications, and a relentless pursuit of innovation. Yet their groundbreaking findings remained confined within academic walls. Why? They never fully grasped the exposure conundrum or understood that reaching a wider audience required a different skill set altogether.

What no one ever told Kiran is this: not only do they need to figure out potential applications and users of their technology, but they must also devise strategies to reach these people and pique their interest. What they *especially* never told Kiran was that none of it is easy. It's not automatic. And that, in today's information-saturated world, the task of capturing audience attention and competing with so many distractions is daunting.

What makes science marketing so complex, and why is it often overlooked? Let's explore some crucial areas where marketing plays a vital role:

1. **Grant funding:** Funding is the lifeblood of research, and competition for grants is fierce. What if you could articulate your research proposal not just accurately but compellingly? With marketing acumen, you'll learn to present your work

in a way that resonates with grant committees and other funders, bringing your crucial research one step closer to fruition.

2. **Venture capital and commercialization:** And what about those trailblazing scientists looking to bridge the gap between innovation and commercialization? Venture capital can seem like a hard nut to crack. But with a dash of marketing flair, you can present your ideas in a way that's not just scientifically sound but also commercially appealing.

3. **Talent acquisition:** The perks don't stop at funding. In the race to attract top talent, your newfound marketing prowess can make a world of difference. You'll learn to sell your vision, not just your salary package. In a world where the brightest minds are drawn toward exciting narratives and grand missions, your marketing-enhanced pitch could be the decisive factor.

4. **Impact:** Is your goal to see your innovations change the world for the better? Yet, how often do brilliant scientific products fall by the wayside, unable to find their way into the hands that need them most? Here's where your marketing skills will shine. By crafting a compelling narrative, you can persuade your target audience and ensure that your innovation becomes a part of people's lives.

SO WHO AM I, ANYWAY?

I was nine years old in 1994. The internet was starting to be "a thing," even in rural Maine. You know that kid who dismantles every gadget in sight? The one whose room looks less like a bedroom and more like an electronics graveyard? Yeah, that was me. Computers, radios, TVs, you name it. I was breaking them apart to see what made them tick. By eleven, I was teaching myself to code and binging internet forums, reveling in all the knowledge at my fingertips and using what I learned to sell server space. My hippie mother called it precociousness. I called it "the way out of Dodge"—or I would have, if I had understood the implications all of this would have.

Conventional education was never a fit for me. All those walls, literal and metaphorical, stifled my eager intellect. While my classmates sat in eighth grade math, I ditched school to immerse myself in university libraries or college lectures. I dropped out of high school at sixteen, enrolling in university full time. Surrounded by future scientists and engineers who struggled to communicate their revolutionary ideas, I saw the immense chasm that existed between great ideas and effective communication. The irony was hard to ignore. It didn't take long for me to realize my calling.

Fast-forward to 2009. I found myself in a very different setting: a packed research center lobby, brimming with anticipation as Dr. Habib Dagher took the stage. As Dagher began to speak, his passion for renewable offshore wind energy and its potential for the State of Maine unfolded persuasively. The audience was captivated.

The parallels between Dagher's performance and those of powerful speakers from myriad fields were unmistakable. They all had the ability to grip an audience, command attention, and leave a lasting impression. This realization sparked a passion in me—a desire to shine a spotlight on scientists who had the power to change the world. Thus, I found my calling in science marketing.

Not long after I saw Dagher speak, I began working for him as a research projects manager—and later as the program manager for Maine's largest R&D program and, later still, the director of global communications for his research center. My science marketing journey was an exhilarating roller-coaster ride, filled with high-speed turns, unexpected drops, and breathtaking peaks.

Unfortunately, the resources available for science-specific marketing at that time were sparse. I didn't have the words for it yet, but I wasn't getting results from traditional marketing and science communications best practices. Despite my best efforts, I found myself learning through trial and error and seeking guidance from the best science marketers I could find. My science marketing education was a cycle of strategizing, executing, and learning from victories and mistakes.

I've since gone on to create a career in science marketing—today I'm the CEO of High Touch Group, one of the handful of marketing agencies that specialize in the field—but it's these experiences and struggles as a novice science marketer that inspired me to write this book. I want to provide a lifeline to new science marketers who, like me many years ago, are passionate about the work but lack the resources to effectively market their scientific products. I hope to provide them—*you*—with a tested method to develop brand and marketing strategies that yield results: customers, media interest, funding, and more.

READY. SET. GO.

Deeply understanding marketing, as with any field, is a lifelong effort, and even the basics can take years to master. But what if we could provide a more direct route to the shoulders of marketing giants? Say, perhaps—a giant's ladder?

This book is that ladder. It's designed to be a practical manual to the distinct discipline of science marketing. It's tailored for those facing the challenges of the exposure conundrum. I wrote it with the following readers in mind:

1. *Visionary scientists, engineers, researchers, and innovators* who are at the helm of start-ups or growing companies. They're eager to foster innovation and growth in an increasingly competitive environment, yet might lack the know-how to effectively communicate about their scientific products or services. The majority of you belong to this group.

2. *Dedicated marketers* tasked with the unique objective of presenting intricate scientific products, services, or research to a broader audience. They're in pursuit of strategies that transcend routine marketing advice and address the specific details of science communication.

3. *Individuals within scientific organizations* who, despite having no background in marketing, find themselves wearing the hat of "marketing coordinator" in addition to their regular duties. (I see you!)

4. *Early career professionals* who find themselves disenchanted by traditional marketing wisdom, yearning to uncover a trove of fresh approaches, custom-built for the sciences.

5. *Enthusiasts, educators, and champions of science communication* who strive to ignite the public's passion, knowledge, and engagement in scientific discovery and application, whose efforts could be supported by science marketing strategies and tactics. If you are aiming to persuade, not just educate, you may find this book useful.

Simply put: if you are tasked with communicating the value of scientific research, products, or services, you are now a "science marketer." Congratulations—I anoint you.

This book is intended as a practical guide—the type of resource I wish I had when I was starting out. But it's also a call to arms of sorts: our world needs more strong science marketers. We face massive global challenges that all might be solved with scientific innovation. From climate change and energy security to global public health and curing disease, the challenges facing scientists are incredible. We need to do better at getting scientific discoveries and innovations to the people who can leverage them to solve these problems, persuade decision makers and influencers, and attract the next generation of innovators.

Above all, we'll embark on a fascinating journey as we ascend the giant's ladder. OK then—let's get started.

RUNG 1

SETTING THE STAGE FOR SCIENCE MARKETING SUCCESS

We'll start by addressing the elephant in the room: you don't have time to absorb every detail about marketing. Your lab, project, or venture doesn't afford you the luxury of spending days perusing marketing textbooks or binging YouTube. And yet, in this intensely competitive climate, it's imperative that your marketing game be stronger than 90 percent of your competition.

This calls for a sharp focus on the practical aspects of marketing, even at the risk of giving short shrift to some theoretical underpinnings that marketing veterans use daily. My goal is to swiftly equip you with the essential skills for marketing your research or innovation. In this spirit, we'll provide a rapid overview of marketing's recent history and the fundamental principles of effective marketing. Then we'll immediately launch into your next actionable steps.

THE HISTORY OF MARKETING: A BRIEF GLIMPSE

The rise of the twentieth century saw the advent of "modern" advertising, where psychological principles were employed to craft compelling messages. These methods laid the foundation for targeted communication that science marketers can use today to convey complex concepts to diverse audiences.

Visionaries such as David Ogilvy and Bill Bernbach revolutionized advertising by viewing it as a creative platform. This era ushered in an understanding that storytelling and emotional engagement are powerful tools—principles that can be leveraged to make scientific innovations resonate with your audiences.

The closing of the twentieth century brought the internet, enabling brands to interact globally and in real time. This digital revolution has also transformed science marketing, opening doors to reach global audiences, whether it's for sharing research, collaboration, or connecting with potential investors and partners.

Enter the era of social media, a dynamic ecosystem that has become a vital part of modern marketing. Science marketing professionals can utilize platforms such as LinkedIn, Twitter, and specialized forums to build communities, share insights, and engage stakeholders in dialogue about research, innovation, and trends.

The essence of effective marketing—understanding human behavior—remains constant. This understanding is also fundamental in science marketing, as it helps to tailor messages that inspire trust, curiosity, and support for scientific endeavors. What motivates a researcher, a healthcare professional, or an investor? How can science marketers tap into these motivations to drive engagement with research, technologies, or products?

As we move forward, we'll explore how these historical marketing principles have been adapted to the unique challenges and opportunities of science marketing, bridging the gap between scientific innovation and market success.

IDENTIFYING YOUR TARGET AUDIENCE

Every successful marketer knows their audience. Good marketing is, at its core, clear communication. If you don't know who you're talking to, how do you know what to say or how and where to say it?

THE THREE PILLARS OF SCIENCE MARKETING

There are three fundamental pillars of science marketing: audience identification, frame (a.k.a. "What's in it for me?", or WIFM), and channel leverage. Skipping any of these steps virtually guarantees that you won't break through the exposure conundrum, making it harder to hit your target with the right message and increasing costs. Taking the time to study your audience and their environment, concerns, and motivators allows you to deliver messages accurately, efficiently, and economically.

Let's start with identifying your target audience—in other words, figuring out who needs to know about your specific discovery, or buy your service or product.

A target audience is the specific group of people you intend to reach. Your audience is typically defined by shared characteristics, such as demographics, interests, or needs. Of course—and this is important, so highlight it, underline it, and take a photo and send it

THE TARGET AUDIENCE MUST CONTRIBUTE TO THE GOALS OF YOUR MARKETING EFFORT.

to yourself—*the target audience must contribute to the goals of your marketing effort.*

Let's use a simple example. Say that I'm targeting a scientist—just broadly, a *scientist* of some sort. Without doing any market research at all, I can immediately make inferences with a high probability of success. For instance, I know that this scientist probably:

1. Lives and works in or near a science and technology hub. Cities such as Boston, San Francisco, and Seattle in the US have vibrant communities of scientists due to the concentration of technology and biotechnology companies, prestigious universities, and research institutions. Outside the US, cities such as London, Berlin, Bangalore, and Shanghai are well known for their thriving science communities.

2. Has worked or currently works with researchers from government agencies such as NASA, the European Space Agency, the US National Institutes of Health, a military branch, or the Max Planck Institutes in Germany. Researchers form tight-knit communities where they collaborate and engage in innovative research, and government-funded R&D fuels many scientists' careers.

3. Likely belongs to one or more scientific organizations, such as the American Association for the Advancement of Science, the Royal Society, or the German Research Foundation (DFG). These institutions serve as platforms where scientists across the globe connect, share insights, and collaborate on various projects.

4. Congregates with colleagues in online communities such as ResearchGate, GitHub, BioMed Central, and arXiv, where they can share and discuss research with peers worldwide.

That's all great. But very rarely are we marketing to "scientists" in a vague, general sense. A discovery has been made or a product or service has been developed, and it was done to solve a problem for someone with more specific needs and wants than a "generic scientist." It's a good start, but now we must define our target market even further. Fortunately, this isn't rocket science; we can continue to narrow our target by geography, job title, company, habits, and more. Those job titles might read specific journals, attend certain industry events, and listen to certain podcasts. All of this is great information, and marketers summarize it in a construct called a "persona." Here's an example of what a persona looks like:

DR. ALEX JOHNSON, PHD

DEMOGRAPHICS:

Age: Thirty-five

Location: Boston, Massachusetts

Education: PhD in electrical engineering with a specialization in robotics

Occupation: Robotics engineer at a leading tech company

Background: Dr. Johnson is a career-driven professional who's passionate about robotics and automation. After a successful academic journey, he has transitioned into the corporate world, working with a team of talented engineers in Boston's tech scene.

Behavior patterns: Dr. Johnson often relies on the latest research and scholarly articles to stay informed about advancements in his field. He's an active participant in online scientific communities such as arXiv and ResearchGate, where he shares his work and engages in discussions with peers globally. Despite his busy schedule, he makes time for monthly meetups with local chapters of professional engineering associations.

Motivations and goals: Driven by a relentless pursuit of innovation, Dr. Johnson's goal is to contribute to breakthroughs in robotics that can revolutionize various sectors, including healthcare, manufacturing, and transportation. He aims to make his mark by leading a significant project in his company or perhaps venturing into an entrepreneurial opportunity someday.

You don't need to know Dr. Johnson to do this. He's just a construct—a persona—based on what you know about people who will most benefit from (and buy) your product or service. But drawing on this persona, we can begin to envision an effective strategy for engaging with him. Our understanding of his motivations, goals, and behaviors informs us about where to reach him, how to talk to him, and what will most likely prompt him to participate in beta product testing or accept an invitation to speak at a seminar. You now have the information necessary to wager a guess as to whether your research, product, or service has value to Alex, and how to reach him if it does.

Understanding your target audience is not merely an exercise; it's a strategic imperative. Creating detailed personas like Dr. Johnson's guides marketers in crafting messages that resonate and motivate. These constructs, akin to the mathematical models used in engineering, lay the groundwork for successful marketing campaigns. By investing time in understanding your audience, you build a robust foundation that aligns with your marketing goals, ensuring that your messages reach the right people at the right time. As we move to the next section, we will explore how to translate these insights into actionable marketing strategies tailored to the unique demands of the science and technology sectors.

COMMUNICATING VALUE TO YOUR AUDIENCE

Let's take this strategy a step further.

The story of the Higgs boson discovery at CERN serves as a pivotal illustration of effective science communication and marketing. This landmark in physics confirmed the existence of the Higgs field, a theory that had been in existence for decades, and brought particle physics to global attention.

The implications of the Higgs boson discovery extended beyond the scientific community, reaching governments, potential funders, and the public. This breakthrough confirmed a particle that gives mass to other particles according to the Standard Model of particle physics, helping to complete the model and deepen our understanding of the fundamental structure of the universe.

CERN faced a dual challenge: first, explaining this intricate discovery to fellow scientists and convincing the Nobel committee of its significance; second, persuading government bodies of the ongoing value of a costly project such as the Large Hadron Collider (LHC), even though the immediate technological benefits might not be apparent.

CERN's success lay in their ability to translate complex physics into engaging narratives without losing scientific integrity. By recognizing different audiences and tailoring their message, CERN successfully navigated these challenges, contributing to our understanding of the universe.

Yet the task was not simple. The communication strategy required a careful balance between technical accuracy and accessibility. This required not only a profound understanding of the subject matter but an acute awareness of the needs and expectations of diverse stakeholders. Take the Higgs boson itself, the final puzzle piece in the Standard

Model of particle physics, and potentially the key to understanding the structure of the physical universe. Explaining a new particle that gives mass to others required careful and thoughtful unpacking for different audiences.

CERN's communications team skillfully tackled this multifaceted challenge. For scientists, they delved into the complexities of quantum mechanics. For the general public, they transformed arcane physics into relatable stories of human achievement. In doing so, they not only kept the integrity of the discovery but also ensured that a broad range of research received its due attention.

> **BY ANALYZING YOUR AUDIENCE'S MOTIVATIONS, INTERESTS, AND COMPREHENSION LEVELS, YOU CAN CRAFT MESSAGES THAT RESONATE AND INSPIRE ACTION.**

The lesson here is clear: understanding and meeting the needs of different audiences are critical components of effective communication in science. Whether it's explaining complex discoveries or justifying the significance of costly research, a targeted and tailored approach can pave the way to success. By analyzing your audience's motivations, interests, and comprehension levels, you can craft messages that resonate and inspire action.

This principle is not just relevant for grand discoveries like the Higgs boson. It applies to any scientific communication, whether it's introducing a new product, seeking funding for a project, or simply sharing findings with peers. By aligning your messages with your audience's wavelength, you're one step closer to achieving your marketing and communication goals.

AUDIENCE SEGMENTATION

An "audience segment" refers to a specific group within the broader target audience, each defined by unique characteristics or needs. It's akin to differentiating between various species within a genus in taxonomy; each shares common attributes but has distinct features that set them apart. In marketing, understanding these nuances allows you to tailor your message and strategy to connect more effectively with each subgroup.

CERN's marketing strategy team might identify *particle physicists* and *astrophysicists* as the two most important segments of the "fellow scientists" target audience.

For particle physicists, the messaging might emphasize the implications of the Higgs boson discovery for the Standard Model of particle physics, which is the theoretical framework that describes the fundamental particles and forces of the universe. The messaging might focus on:

1. **The experimental setup and the Large Hadron Collider:** discussing the specifics of the LHC and the detectors, such as ATLAS and the content management system (CMS), that played a crucial role in the discovery.

2. **The role of the Higgs boson in the Standard Model:** explaining how the discovery of the Higgs boson confirms the Higgs field's existence, which is responsible for giving particles mass.

3. **Implications for particle physics research:** detailing the potential impact of the discovery on the understanding of fundamental forces, the search for new particles, and possible extensions or modifications to the Standard Model.

4. **Future experiments and directions:** discussing the prospects for refining the measurements of the Higgs boson's properties and exploring other aspects of particle physics that might arise from the discovery.

For astrophysicists, the messaging might highlight the broader implications of the Higgs boson discovery for understanding the universe's origins, evolution, and fundamental properties. The messaging might focus on:

1. **The Higgs boson and the early universe:** describing the role of the Higgs field in the early universe, its connection to cosmic inflation, and the subsequent formation of structures like galaxies.

2. **Dark matter and dark energy:** exploring the potential links between the Higgs boson discovery and the search for dark matter particles or insights into the nature of dark energy, which are critical components of the universe's composition and evolution.

3. **Implications for cosmology and astrophysics:** discussing the broader impact of the Higgs boson discovery on our understanding of fundamental forces and particles, and how they shape the universe at both small and large scales.

4. **Interdisciplinary research opportunities:** highlighting the potential for collaborations between particle physicists and astrophysicists to further explore the connections between the Higgs boson discovery and various aspects of the cosmos.

Marketers often use terms such as "audience" and "target audience" interchangeably with "segment." In campaign discussions, the meaning is usually clear, but in market studies, these distinctions are crucial. For example, your "audience" might be healthcare professionals, but your "segment" could be oncologists specializing in breast cancer treatment. If ever in doubt, clarify to ensure everyone is on the same page.

In science marketing, the principle "You can't be everything to everyone" is paramount. Precise targeting ensures that your message reaches the right ears, whether it's a groundbreaking discovery or a pioneering technology. Take a moment to reflect on your own audience segmentation strategies. Are you feeding precision leads to your sales team, or are you lost in the exposure conundrum? By homing in on the segments that matter most, you can transform your approach and truly connect with the core of your audience.

WHAT DO THEY WANT? WHAT DO THEY NEED?

You've successfully identified your target market. Great work! Yet understanding your audience goes beyond just identifying them; it means stepping into their shoes, seeing through their eyes, and comprehending their mindset. Specifically, you must discern their value perception—what stirs their decisions and the motivations behind their actions. Put simply, you need to answer their fundamental question: "What's in it for me?"

The answer to the WIFM question must be part of what I like to call the "value vow" (a.k.a. the "value proposition"). It's a precise articulation of the benefits you offer, fine-tuned to align with the specific desires and needs of each distinct audience segment. It's the fulcrum that can pivot a casual observer into an engaged customer or investor.

Discerning your audience's ideal value vow is not always straightforward. Factors such as experience, biases, economic pressures, and societal trends often color their perceptions and decisions. Consequently, understanding these nuances is essential for crafting a resonant message, including your value vow.

Let's imagine you're the founder of a materials science start-up that's discovered a new method of producing highly efficient photovoltaic cells using a blend of organic polymers. Your primary audience consists of potential investors, energy sector clients, and industry regulators. The value vows for each segment must be distinct:

- Potential investors are looking for proof of concept, commercial viability, and a solid return on investment. Questions such as "How does your approach surpass traditional silicon-based photovoltaics? Why invest in your company?" must be addressed, focusing on projected returns and market positioning.

- Meanwhile, for customers in the energy sector, reliability, efficiency, cost-effectiveness, and maintenance ease are key. They'll ask, "How can your solution enhance our clean energy production without escalating costs?" The value vow here must underscore efficiency gains and potential cost savings.

- Finally, the interests of industry regulators are anchored in public welfare, environmental sustainability, and compliance—or they should be. Questions such as "How does your product align with ecological standards for mass implementation?" will be pivotal. Your value vow to this segment should highlight sustainability and adherence to regulatory guidelines and permitting procedures.

This multifaceted approach to the value proposition, analogous to the diverse refractive indices of anisotropic crystals, illustrates the fluid nature of audience perception. It's a dynamic process; these perceptions may evolve alongside changes in your company or the broader industry landscape. Continuously analyzing your audience, understanding their evolving needs, and adjusting your messaging will secure the precision and efficacy of your marketing endeavors.

In summary, the value vow is not a slogan or tagline but a targeted response to your audience segments' central question of "What's in it for me?" It's a critical tool that offers insight into their decision-making core, allowing you to craft messaging that truly connects.

CRAFTING THE RIGHT MESSAGE

Think of a marketing message as a precision-engineered tool, crafted to connect with a specific audience—your target market—and to provoke a reaction. It's a succinct, incisive statement that conveys the unique benefits of your product, service, or brand. The ultimate aim of a marketing message is to distill the essential attributes of what you're offering, aligning them with the interests and needs of your audience, thereby shaping their decisions and urging them to act.

To resonate, an influential science marketing message should be:

1. **Comprehensible:** the message must be easily understood, devoid of technical jargon, and articulate the core value vow succinctly.
2. **Relevant:** the content must align with the specific needs, ambitions, or obstacles confronting your target audience.
3. **Compelling:** the message should evoke emotion or curiosity, or foster a sense of urgency, leading the audience to engage.
4. **Distinctive:** to stand out among competitors, the message should underscore exclusive advantages and distinct attributes.

5. **Consistent:** uniformity across various channels and assets fortifies the brand's identity and maintains the integrity of the overall messaging strategy.

How do we synthesize these elements into an effective message? The technique lies in framing.

Framing refers to the contextualization of information to influence decisions. How could we incorporate framing into our hypothetical materials science start-up's messaging? Here's an example:

Advance the clean energy frontier with our innovative organic photovoltaic cells. Comprising a unique polymer blend, our technology delivers superior efficiency at reduced production costs. Engage in the green revolution now, and embrace a sustainable, profitable future with us.

This message maintains clarity and distinction while adding an impetus for action. It accentuates the exclusive benefits of your product and the pressing need for sustainable energy solutions. It's more than just words; it's a strategically crafted appeal that, if communicated effectively, can resonate deeply with your audience and imprint your brand upon their consciousness.

The craft of messaging isn't confined to its creation. Equally critical is pinpointing the best channels and methods to convey that message, especially to a multifaceted audience like that in a scientific community. Here, understanding the diverse characteristics and preferences of your audience segments plays a vital role in ensuring that the message not only reaches its destination but also makes an impactful connection.

WHICH CHANNEL TO CHOOSE?

Selecting the appropriate channels to convey your message is a critical step following target identification and message refinement. Marketing channels are the conduits that connect you, the message creator, with your desired audience, enabling you to bridge the gap between your offering and those who would benefit from it. These channels encompass a wide range, including traditional media, digital platforms, live events, academic journals, conferences, and more. The secret lies in knowing where your target audience frequents and what they trust.

When defining your audience, you likely invested time in developing "personas" to understand who your customers are, what influences them, their preferences, habits, and trust factors. An integral part of this process involves identifying where your targets obtain their information, including traditional media, influencers, podcasts, social networks, and specialized channels.

Take, for example, our hypothetical materials start-up's marketing team. They may leverage industry-specific webinars and technical conferences not for immediate promotion but to delve deeper into understanding their audience. Analyzing professional affiliations, social media activity, and reading preferences can reveal the optimal channels to communicate with this group.

Consider these aspects:

- Does visibility at an industry event enhance credibility?
- Will publishing a technical white paper foster confidence among potential partners or investors?
- Could a webinar hosted by a respected materials science journal or industry association serve your goals?

These insights help us allocate our marketing resources most efficiently and build out more detailed audience personas.

Marketing channels can be further classified into three primary categories:

- Paid media: traditional advertising, including print, radio, TV, direct mail, paid search, event sponsorships, etc.
- Owned media: channels directly under your control, such as websites, blogs, social media, and trade show exhibits.
- Earned media: exposure gained through nonpaid methods, such as word of mouth, social media mentions, forums, review sites, press coverage, and peer reviews.

But what if you're new to a field—say, genomics—and need to identify appropriate marketing channels? There are several ways to find relevant marketing channels:

- Network with professionals for recommendations.
- Identify leading academic journals, trade publications, and blogs.
- Seek key conferences, workshops, and online communities.
- Discover influential individuals or organizations with robust social media presence.

Understanding your target's interest areas, from genomics to renewable energy or neuroscience, is essential. Consider the unique attributes and goals of each target within that field to guide your selection of marketing channels.

For instance, if you are targeting prospects in the genomics field, you might have different groups of targets including researchers, biotechnology companies, and investors. Targeting each group through different channels may be most effective:

- **Researchers:** academic journals, conferences, webinars, and platforms such as ResearchGate or GitHub.
- **Biotechnology companies:** industry publications, networking events, online forums, and specialized platforms such as LinkedIn.
- **Investors:** professional networks, technology incubators, research conferences, and publication history.

Selecting the right channels requires an in-depth understanding of your audience and an astute awareness of where they consume information. It's about reaching your audience in a manner that resonates and compels them to action.

By investing time and resources into identifying your audience, understanding their ideal value vow, crafting a compelling message, and choosing the right channels to reach them, you set the stage for a successful science marketing campaign. Remember, the better you understand your audience and how to reach them, the more effective your marketing efforts will be.

KEY TAKEAWAYS

1. The foundation of effective science marketing lies in a deep understanding of your target audience. This involves identifying who they are; understanding their concerns, fundamental motivations, and preferences; and discovering where they congregate.

2. Effective communication is about crafting resonant messages that inspire action, tailored to meet the specific needs and wants of each audience segment. Framing is a key tool in this process, aiding the construction of a core message that highlights the benefits of your offering or the consequences of not adopting it.

3. A well-planned marketing strategy allows for accurate, efficient, and economical delivery of your messaging, preventing wasted resources and ineffective communication. This includes understanding your audience's WIFM question and answering it effectively.

4. The concept of a "value vow" serves as a unique promise of the benefits your scientific innovation provides. Recognizing the dynamic nature of value vows, influenced by factors such as experiences, biases, economic pressures, and societal trends, and adapting your communication strategy to the evolving needs of your audience are critical.

5. The selection of appropriate marketing channels is crucial to delivering your message effectively. Channels should be chosen based on their relevance to your audience and field.

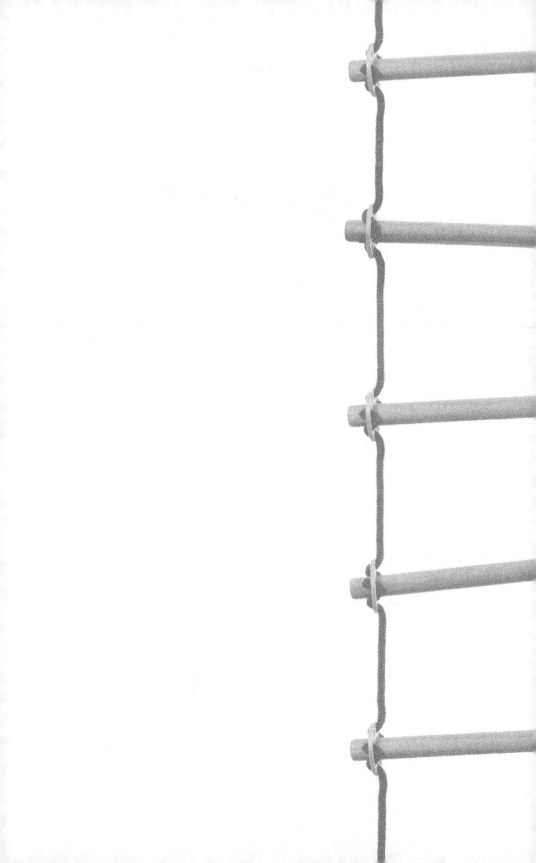

FROM PRODUCT TO NARRATIVE: THE SCIENCE OF STORYTELLING

When I was six years old, I tried to sell my brother on the side of the road.

This is true.

My brother and I are separated by a mere three years—a seemingly gargantuan gap in our early days. To my young mind, this interloper was siphoning off what was rightfully mine—the undivided attention of my family. (It's only fair to note—and I'm sure he'd agree—that he was a child with decibel levels that could rival a jet engine and usually came at you armed with a plastic sword.)

The talk of the playground around that time was that the local convenience store had started selling boxes of Jolly Ranchers for $5. One afternoon, I hatched a plan to kill two birds at once: I fastened him into his car seat, set him at the edge of our quiet country road, and hoisted a sign that enthusiastically announced, "Boy for Sale: $5." I brimmed with anticipation of the financial windfall.

Minutes passed, as did the cars. Maybe my sign needed a better description. I grabbed my marker. "Gross Boy for Sale: $5." It was certainly more honest, but still—no interested buyers.

Maybe he was too expensive, I thought. I had no idea how much brothers should cost—*I* didn't buy him—but I knew that I needed $5 for those Jolly Ranchers. I sighed and picked up the marker again: "Gross Boy for Sale: $4.50." After this deep of a discount, someone had to want him, I reasoned.

Unfortunately, my prospective customers kept driving by.

I looked at the sign again for something to change. No, it was perfect. The problem had to be *him*. I fixed his hair, wiped a smear off his cheek, handed him a teddy bear, and backed up to survey my work. Not a major improvement, but it would have to do. Several cars slowed down, but to my chagrin, nobody stopped.

Suddenly, I had an epiphany: nobody can see my sign until it is too late! What if I put up another sign that just said "Sale!" a few feet from the driveway? That way drivers know to stop before they get to my shop. Brilliant!

Within minutes of enacting this strategy, a man stopped and asked, "Is the sale in the house?"

"No, it's right here," I replied and pointed at my brother.

He looked at me, the sign, my brother napping in his car seat, and back to me. "Is your mother home?"

Much to my surprise, not a single dollar made its way to me that day. More fortuitously, neither did child protective services. The details of how that day ended are a bit fuzzy, but the story lives on as a family tale about the day I nearly brokered my brother to a stranger.

This whimsical memory from my childhood illustrates an early lesson in marketing that continues to influence my work to this day. I had a clear goal, a product to sell, and a price in mind. What I lacked was an understanding of the value vow—in this case, that there wasn't one—market positioning, and most importantly, a compelling narrative.

Let's delve into these concepts:

- **Value vow:** I knew what I wanted ($5 for Jolly Ranchers) but failed to understand the value of my offering to potential customers. As we discussed in the last chapter, understanding the unique benefits and importance of a product or research can make or break your marketing efforts.
- **Market positioning:** Putting my brother on the side of the road with a hastily made sign was far from an optimal strategy. Understanding where and how to position a product, such as a new medical device, requires analyzing the target audience, competition, and market dynamics.

> **A WELL-CRAFTED NARRATIVE CAN TURN A COMPLEX IDEA INTO AN ACCESSIBLE AND APPEALING CONCEPT.**

- **Crafting a compelling narrative:** Finally, my failure to craft a compelling narrative that resonated with potential customers resulted in zero sales. As you'll learn in this chapter, a well-crafted narrative can turn a complex idea into an accessible and appealing concept.

AN IN-DEPTH EXPLORATION OF PRODUCT

You're probably not reading this book for tips on how to sell your sibling. More likely, you're facing the new or unavoidable responsibility of marketing your scientific product or that of your organization. You might be feeling overwhelmed, and that's perfectly OK. Let's ease into this by running through the typical stages of a new science marketing project.

First, some quick definitions. In this book, when we use the term "product," we're referring to either a product *or* a service that needs to be marketed. When we say "stakeholder" we mean anyone with a vested interest in the success of this product. That includes you.

THE KICKOFF MEETING

The project typically begins with a kickoff meeting, an essential stage that sets the tone for everything that follows. Whether you're an inventor, CEO, or the sole member of your organization, this process matters. It's a time to align everyone involved and uncover crucial information needed for success.

Here are the questions that should be answered so you can understand the product in greater detail:

- What is our goal for this project? Usually the answer is "Sales!" but some people in the meeting might say, "We want more website traffic" or "We want more brand awareness." Sometimes the answer is simply, "We just want people to care about this."

- Who are we trying to reach? Who buys our product? Who do we want to buy the product? In "marketing-ese," we are asking for the target audience. When speaking to other stakeholders, such as a sales team or the CEO, this is usually better asked with language such as "Who are we talking to?" or "Who are we selling to?"

- Tell me more about the audience. Why do they need our product? Do they already know who we are? What do they think about us? What's causing that perception? How do you know? What else would be helpful to know about this audience? Do we have any research (e.g., surveys, focus groups, or secondary market research reports) that might be helpful as we get to know the target audience?

- What do we want the target audience to do after they hear about or interact with our product?

- Is this a brand-new marketing effort for this product? If not, what else have we tried? What were the results? How do we know? What did we learn from the results?

- What else is new in this market/product category/industry? This gives you the opportunity to talk about a competitor's product launch, or recent advances in the industry. What will your competitors do after this product is launched? Are there any changes in the market that make your product more relevant? Are your closest competitors doing anything similar or interesting right now?

- What makes this product/service/company unique? Can we share any news as part of this effort? You are looking for anything that is first, last, new, or different.

- What is the time frame for delivering on this project's goals? Very often, there is a countdown to a product launch, funding milestone, or other event that is driving the deadline. Figure out what is affecting the timeline for projects.

- What is the project or account budget? What, if anything, has claimed part of the budget already? For example, has there already been a media buy associated with a product launch? Has a booth already been purchased for a conference? Be clear on where the budget stands.

- What assets and resources already exist? This could run the gamut of scientific leadership available for content creation interviews or to offer up to journalists as subject matter experts, or b-roll or professional photography. You'll need to do a detailed intake of these assets as part of the briefing process. Get a contact for who can help with that within the account.

- For projects without an established approval chain, find out who needs to review and approve strategy and assets. Often, these are different people. For new projects with a lot of assets, find out if the primary contact is adding any additional reviewers or approvals to that chain. Be sure to follow up for contact details to include in the brief (at least names, titles, emails, phone numbers, and usual time zones).

- Are there any "must-haves" for this account or project? Some of these might flow out naturally as the conversation continues, but someone should always ask the specific question, regardless. Examples might include trademarks, specific logos for the product, calls to action, and final deliverable formats, if known.

- Less of a question than your own "must-have": try to figure out who your various points of communication are on the project. This might include a knowledgeable sales team member who can get you customer insights, an overview of the sales cycle, sales data, and other important information; an admin type who can collect marketing assets, old ads, and any existing market research or plans; and a technical lead who can get you applicable published research, detailed product information, a lab tour, and other scientific information that might be helpful that may not be immediately accessible. Be sure to also include any "watch-outs" for you and your team, such as a VIP's oddly spelled last name.

PRODUCT UNDERSTANDING

It's probably useful to pause here and talk about product marketing management more generally. In science marketing, we often deal with organizations that have many products. At High Touch Group, one life sciences tools client has more than twenty thousand individual products—and that's not unheard of nor even that large compared to other companies in that space. Another has fifty, and yet another has only a single product with three variations. If your project involves many different products, your questions might require more complexity, but the gist is the same: before you can adequately market a product, you need to understand your product offering and the scope of what you're working with.

The process for understanding clients' products and services that we use at High Touch Group is as rigorous as our process for identifying their target audiences (you'll read more about this in the next chapter). We start with a simple intake process, asking variations on the questions we just walked through. If we've been retained to launch or create marketing programs for multiple products or services, we'll complete intake processes for each one. It's important to understand how a company's product and/or service lines are interrelated, or if a new product is, in fact, an update or replacement of a product with an established market presence.

If it's an existing product, we collect every piece of marketing material ever produced for it, including

- product assets such as professional photography, videography, and product-specific branding, such as logos, trademarks, and messaging;
- collateral, which might include sales presentations, brochures, case studies, white papers, and catalogs;

- product packaging and packaging requirements, such as labeling requirements;
- back-end access to websites, social media accounts, customer relationship management (CRM) systems, marketing automation platforms, and associated analytics;
- a list of tradeshows or other events where the client has demoed or otherwise showcased the product or plans to, and any documented results from those events; and
- any relevant publications and conference proceedings, which might be about the product directly or could use the product and name it in a materials and methods section, or similar.

In other words, we gather everything and anything that has been employed and deployed to explain, promote, and persuade trial and purchase. We also note important gaps, such as product photography and messaging consistency.

We'll usually request that we receive a sample of the product, if feasible. This is especially important for early asset creation if professional photos do not already exist. We request to receive it the same way a customer would—in the same packaging and delivered the same way. For example, we might document the process of opening and inspecting the product's packaging, taking detailed notes about what could be improved.

If we're marketing a service or capability, we'll do a site walkthrough with the client where we have access to their scientists, technologists, and engineers at all phases of their work. We ask to sit in on customer calls to gain insight into their target audience. If we're lucky, the client will trust us enough to let us interview their customers (or at least survey them).

In my experience, the values and benefits are rarely expressed in terms of mere improvement. Often, our clients are directly confronting established practices. The objective of their product, service, or process—the "why" of it—may be to change accepted practice and, by default, change the behavior of the target market. We ask for comparisons or explanations about how a product or service is used or delivered versus how it's done *without* the product or service. What niche need does it fill?

We'll dig into the founder's story to determine if it belongs in the overall messaging. Can it be used to engage interest or generate excitement? What problem were they trying to solve? How did they come up with that idea? Developing a positive, invested relationship with the scientist, originator, inventor, or product development team during this due diligence phase helps build trust and a sense of partnership.

KNOWING THE LANDSCAPE: DEFINING THE COMPETITION

In science marketing, competition transcends the conventional notion of rival businesses offering similar products or services. It embraces a broader spectrum, encompassing not only direct competitors but also indirect challenges such as ingrained industry attitudes, technological hurdles, and barriers to change. For instance, competition may arise from well-established practices within an industry that resist innovation or a pervasive mindset that perceives new methodologies as unnecessary risks.

Understanding competition in this expanded sense is vital for developing effective marketing strategies. Let's explore this concept by examining a hypothetical high-strength composite materials start-up, a company that confronts not only competing products but also entrenched beliefs and standards within its target industries.

This hypothetical company develops high-strength composite materials that can replace traditional metals in various applications, from construction to manufacturing. Now imagine an industry reliant on conventional metal materials for its products, viewing the switch to high-strength composites as risky or unnecessary. This traditional approach might result in continued high production costs, increased energy consumption, and potential environmental impacts. However, transitioning to innovative composites could offer lower production costs, increased efficiency, and improved environmental sustainability. Nonetheless, this shift challenges the industry to alter long-standing practices and introduce new processes.

In this scenario, the competitor isn't another company producing high-strength composites. It isn't even a substitute product. The competitor is an ingrained mindset, and this intangible factor can obstruct your marketing efforts.

Defining the competition in science marketing demands a holistic view of the landscape, incorporating both direct competitors and the hurdles that inhibit progress and innovation. It involves pinpointing the market forces, established attitudes, and outmoded practices that may stand in the way of a product's or service's success. By acknowledging these factors, marketers can position their offerings strategically, surmounting obstacles that restrict growth and market penetration.

In the next section, we'll delve further into crafting a persuasive value vow that distinguishes your product or service from the competition, enabling you to establish your unique space in the marketplace.

VALUE VOW, REVISITED

In chapter 1, I introduced the concept of the "value vow," a crucial element of your product's ultimate story. In essence, the value vow is the tool we use to communicate to potential customers why they should purchase a product or do business with a particular company. Its purpose is to clearly highlight the unique benefits of the product or service from the very first impression or point of contact. We want customers to think, "Here's my need, and here's the product or service that fulfills it."

The value vow serves as a guide for developing all marketing materials, including advertisements and trade show booth signage. The value vow is specific to different target audiences, meaning that if a product offers varying values to different segments, a unique value vow should be crafted for each audience.

Here are the five key attributes that a good value vow should possess:

- It should be easy to understand and relate to.
- It should communicate the tangible results that end users can expect from using the product or service.
- It should differentiate the offering in the marketplace by emphasizing a distinct and superior benefit, such as cost or time efficiency, ease of use, or other key features.
- It should utilize language that instills confidence, conveys honesty, and avoids jargon, slang, or hype that could diminish the message. Using respectful and educated language enhances the credibility of the message.

- It should establish a visceral connection with the target audience and convey the value proposition in five seconds or less.

To develop the value vow, we begin by asking ourselves and the stakeholders, "What are the three characteristics or features of the company, product, or service that contribute to delivering the end user benefit?" Although there may be numerous features, it is important to map each one to an end benefit. If a feature does not align with a specific benefit, it may not add value to the key messaging but could indicate a differentiation point from competitors. Additionally, it is essential to recognize that while many features and benefits may overlap among audience segments, not every feature will be equally important or valued by every potential customer.

Let's return to the hypothetical example of the materials start-up producing high-strength composites. The benefits derived from such materials will vary for a small construction company focusing on local projects compared to a multinational manufacturing conglomerate that has production facilities across the globe. For the conglomerate, the emphasized features might include durability, consistency in material performance, significant cost reductions, improved sustainability, and the ability to scale production. Conversely, for the smaller construction company, the value proposition would shift, placing emphasis on the lightweight nature of the materials, ease of use, improved safety standards, and the potential for improved project timelines and profitability. In other words, the value vow for the same product may be different for different clients.

Differentiation is an essential aspect of positioning your product or service uniquely in the marketplace. In science marketing, where offerings may have overlapping features or cater to niche sectors, it's especially vital to delineate what sets your product or service apart. Here are specific techniques to achieve that differentiation:

1. **Identify unique selling propositions (USPs):** Determine the unique features or benefits that separate your product or service from competitors. It may be a patented technology, unparalleled efficiency, or specific customization options. Emphasizing these USPs in marketing collateral can create a distinct identity.

2. **Understand your audience's pain points:** By deeply understanding the problems, concerns, or needs of your target audience, you can tailor your offering to provide specialized solutions. Addressing these pain points directly can make your product or service more appealing compared to generic alternatives.

3. **Emphasize quality and value:** If your product or service provides a higher-quality solution, even at a premium price, showcasing this quality and explaining the long-term value can set you apart. For example, in the field of composites, highlighting how a material's strength and durability translate into cost savings over time could be a key differentiator.

4. **Showcase expertise and credibility:** Leveraging your team's expertise, certifications, or affiliations can establish authority in the field. Highlighting case studies, research collaborations, or industry recognition can further enhance your unique position.

5. **Create tailored solutions:** In industries such as automation or life sciences, providing customized solutions can be a strong differentiator. By working closely with clients to understand their unique requirements and developing

solutions that cater precisely to those needs, you can establish a reputation for personalized service and innovation.

6. **Use storytelling to connect:** Often, the technical nature of scientific products may overshadow the human impact. By narrating real-world applications and success stories, you can form a connection with your audience that goes beyond specifications and features.

By embracing these techniques, science marketers can not only differentiate their products and services but also create a more resonant and meaningful connection with potential customers. Recognizing that differentiation is more than just contrasting features, but a comprehensive understanding of value, quality, and alignment with your audience's needs, can lead to more compelling and successful messaging.

A QUICK NOTE ON TEAM MANAGEMENT

It's entirely possible that you're marketing a product alone like some kind of scientific ronin. It's equally possible that you're managing a team, whether a formal one or a committee assembled specifically for this task. If the latter applies to you, the team will probably be starting its work in earnest around this time. Here are a few pointers I'd like to offer based on my years of experience:

- **Emphasize the importance of notetaking:** Stress the significance of notetaking during meetings, especially when engaging with other stakeholders or attending critical sessions like the kickoff call. Good notetaking ensures that important information and insights are captured accurately, aiding in the project's success. Model the behavior of taking thorough notes and reinforce the expectation for all team members to do the same.

- **Clearly define roles and responsibilities:** Ensure that each team member has a clear understanding of their role and responsibilities within the project. Clearly define the scope of their tasks and expectations, which will help establish accountability and avoid confusion.

- **Foster effective communication:** Encourage open and transparent communication within the team. Establish regular check-ins or meetings to discuss progress, address any challenges, and share updates. Utilize collaborative tools and platforms to streamline communication and facilitate easy access to relevant project information.

Remember, effective team management involves setting clear expectations, promoting communication and collaboration, and addressing any issues or challenges promptly. By fostering a supportive and organized team environment, you can enhance productivity and the overall success of marketing a science product.

CRAFTING THE NARRATIVE: BUILDING THE BRAND STORY

At this stage, you are prepared to construct your brand story. A good brand story serves as the defining narrative for the company and its products or services. It goes beyond simply stating facts and features; it provides the creative team with insight into the emotional nuances that resonate with the target audience. Building a compelling brand story is

A GOOD BRAND STORY SERVES AS THE DEFINING NARRATIVE FOR THE COMPANY AND ITS PRODUCTS OR SERVICES.

indeed a challenging task that requires a deep understanding of and appreciation for the product. When crafting a brand story, several key elements should be considered:

- **Founder's story and mission statement:** The brand story should incorporate the founder's story, their motivation, and the mission statement of the company. This helps establish a connection between the brand and its audience by showcasing the passion and purpose behind the product or service.
- **Knitting together assets:** The brand story should weave together all the assets gathered thus far. It should synthesize the key messages, value vows, target audience insights, and competitive differentiators into a cohesive narrative.
- **Speaking of value…:** The brand story should *emphasize* the value that the product or service brings to the customer's life. It should clearly communicate how the offering solves a problem, fulfills a need, or improves the customer's experience. This value should be articulated in a way that resonates with the target audience.
- **Targeting a specific audience:** The brand story should be tailored to a specific audience or customer segment. By understanding the needs, aspirations, and pain points of the target audience, the brand story can effectively connect with them on an emotional level.

Like marketing other disciplines, science marketers approach brand storytelling as standard narrative arcs that feature conflict (pain points), key characters (founders/innovators), target audience, and, in the middle of it all, the product as the hero. An examination of the challenges that the founders and innovators overcame helps leverage their stories to appeal to potential customers, showcasing the journey toward scientific breakthroughs. We consider the end user and envision how the product or service can make a meaningful difference in their lives. The best brand stories tap into the emotions that need to be evoked in the target audience, establishing a genuine connection.

PERSONIFICATION IN BRANDING: BRINGING THE PRODUCT TO LIFE

One of the most intriguing and effective ways to build a brand story is to utilize personification. This approach involves attributing humanlike characteristics to the product or service, allowing the audience to relate to it on a more personal and emotional level. Here's how you can effectively use personification in your brand story:

1. **Identify key traits**: Determine the most essential and appealing characteristics of the product or service. Is it strong and reliable, or sleek and innovative? What human qualities best represent those characteristics?

2. **Create a character profile**: Develop a complete character profile that represents your product or service. Consider factors such as appearance, personality, behaviors, and values. What would this character do in a typical day? How would it interact with others?

3. **Connect with the target audience**: Align the personified character with the needs and aspirations of the target audience. If the product is designed for a tech-savvy audience, the character might be portrayed as an intelligent and forward-thinking innovator.

4. **Weave into storytelling**: Integrate the character into your overall brand narrative. It could be featured in marketing campaigns, storytelling videos, or user experiences. This

character becomes a consistent symbol of what the brand stands for.

5. **Keep it consistent**: Ensure that the personification is maintained consistently across all marketing channels and touchpoints. This consistency reinforces the brand's identity and makes it more memorable.

6. **Evaluate and evolve**: As with other aspects of branding, the personification should be reviewed and updated as needed to align with changing market trends and customer perceptions.

Consider our hypothetical materials start-up producing high-strength composites. By personifying the product as an innovative engineer who always seeks to build things better, more efficiently, and in an environmentally friendly manner, the brand can create an image that resonates with engineers, construction companies, and environmentalists alike. This character might be portrayed in marketing materials as an animated figure, with visual and verbal cues that convey innovation, reliability, and concern for sustainability. Such an approach not only adds depth to the brand's story but also creates an engaging and relatable experience for the target audience.

By carefully crafting this personified image, science marketers can make a complex or abstract product more tangible and relatable. Personification becomes a unique tool to convey the brand's values, mission, and unique selling proposition, connecting on an emotional level and creating a distinctive brand identity in the market.

ITERATION

Once the brand story is approved, it is handed off to someone with the vision, tools, and talent to make it "real" (i.e., develop a brand identity). Depending on your organization, you may have a creative services team that is responsible for the development of foundational assets such as the logo, mission and value statements, taglines, and web resources, among other foundational elements. Your organization may lack an in-house marketing department, or you may have assumed the role of "marketing coordinator," a title that may not fully encapsulate your responsibilities. It is essential to recognize the development of a brand story that informs a larger brand identity as a significant advancement. This achievement distinguishes your efforts from many others and represents a meaningful progression in your marketing strategy development.

However, constructing a brand story and identity is far from a one-time endeavor. It is, in fact, a dynamic and iterative process that requires continuous assessment, adaptation, and refinement. The iterative process recognizes that the market landscape, consumer preferences, technological advancements, and even the products or services themselves are subject to change.

Here's how iteration is typically integrated into building the brand story:

1. **Initial development:** Start with a comprehensive understanding of the company's mission, the product's unique value, target audience insights, and competitive landscape. Create the initial brand narrative and identity that encapsulates these key elements.

2. **Testing and feedback:** Once the brand story has been crafted, it should be tested with internal stakeholders, focus groups, or a segment of the target audience. Gathering feedback at this stage ensures that the brand resonates with the intended audience and aligns with the company's core values.

3. **Analysis and refinement:** Based on the feedback received, necessary adjustments should be made to the brand story

and visual elements. This phase focuses on fine-tuning the message, enhancing the emotional connection, and reinforcing the unique "value vow."

4. **Implementation:** After the refinement, the updated brand elements are implemented across various marketing channels, aligning all communication to the cohesive brand story.

5. **Ongoing evaluation and adaptation:** The process does not end with implementation. Regular monitoring, analysis, and adaptation are vital to ensure that the brand continues to resonate with the target audience and reflect the evolving nature of the market and product. The iterative process allows for ongoing adjustments and enhancements that keep the brand fresh, relevant, and competitive.

By embracing iteration, science marketers create a living brand story that evolves alongside the company, products, and market dynamics. It fosters agility, allowing for rapid response to new opportunities or challenges and ensuring that the brand remains in sync with the ever-changing landscape of science and technology. This approach recognizes that a brand is not a static entity but a dynamic one, capable of growth, transformation, and continued relevance.

In the next chapter, we'll delve into the process of synthesizing all the gathered information and insights into a cohesive marketing strategy.

KEY TAKEAWAYS

1. Understanding your competitive landscape involves a lot more than just knowing your direct competitors. Indirect competitors—those that solve your customers' problems in different ways—also matter. Consider any substitutes or alternatives that your customers might consider instead of your product. In addition, be aware of potential competitors that could enter your market in the future. A comprehensive competitive analysis will help you understand these various factors.

2. Your overarching value vow should be appealing enough to all segments, while the segment-specific messages should address the unique needs and priorities of each group. This ensures that your value proposition is consistent across all your marketing materials, which strengthens your overall brand.

3. It's essential to consider user experience when crafting your brand story. Think about how your customers interact with your product or service and the journey they take from discovery to purchase and beyond. Incorporate these elements into your brand story to make it more relatable and engaging.

BLUEPRINTS FOR SUCCESS: STRATEGY DEVELOPMENT IN SCIENCE MARKETING

As I mentioned earlier, I was fortunate early in my career to join forces with Dr. Habib Dagher at the University of Maine's Advanced Structures and Composites Center (ASCC). Among our many projects, the DeepCwind program stood out for its immense potential to impact climate change—an issue paramount to every lifeform on this planet.

The initiative aimed to combat climate change by developing floating offshore wind platforms, laying groundwork for electrical grid infrastructure and improving permitting process. Dr. Dagher's goal was ambitious: reinvigorating Maine's economy with an estimated private capital influx of $20 billion, creating over ten thousand jobs, and reducing greenhouse gas emissions.

I was all in.

A STRATEGIC CHALLENGE

The DeepCwind initiative was structured around three primary value vows:

1. **Economic development:** spurring job creation in various sectors and rejuvenating coastal communities with new employment opportunities
2. **Energy independence:** reducing Maine's dependence on fossil fuels by harnessing wind energy offshore, providing a stable, locally controlled power supply
3. **Environmental stewardship:** investing in renewable energy sources such as offshore wind to reduce dependence on fossil fuels, serving as a blueprint for other parts of the world

This program had an important milestone to achieve: Maine needed to demonstrate itself as the state capable of leading this nationwide initiative. With an aging population and young engineers leaving the state for employment, Maine needed more resident engineers and skilled technicians.

The Windstorm Challenge was among several initiatives supporting this aspect of the program. We conducted hands-on workshops in schools, using a traveling wind-wave tank to teach students about offshore wind power. Collaboration with the Maine School of Science and Mathematics led to the Windstorm Challenge, inviting students across the state to design a floating turbine system and develop a business plan. The competition provided scholarships, internships, and invaluable experience, reaching thousands of students and bringing deepwater offshore wind research into thousands of Maine households.

Transparently, not every person in every community agreed that deepwater offshore wind was the right solution for Maine. At times, there was opposition. However, virtually everyone agreed that Maine needed more jobs for its young people. This was particularly evident in the communities most deeply tied to Maine's traditional industries, such as fishing and forestry. Parents were deeply concerned about the future of these industries for their kids, and rightly so. On many evenings, my team sat around kitchen tables listening to stories about how the cod—the fish themselves and the catches—used to be large, but "not anymore." They knew that between overfishing, climate change, and increasing regulation, their children and grandchildren needed other options. The offshore wind program needed engineers and skilled technicians. This opened an opportunity for us to engage with a younger generation.

As of this writing, the Windstorm Challenge is still going strong. The program has reached thousands of students in all corners of the state. Importantly, many of its participants have gone on to study engineering at the University of Maine and intern as part of the offshore wind program. But it also did something that millions of advertising dollars would have struggled to accomplish: it brought deepwater offshore wind research (our "product") into the homes of Maine citizens. Between in-school workshops from the traveling wind-wave tank, tours of the ASCC, and the Windstorm Challenge, a commendable portion of the state's K–12 population had been reached. The program also received attention from state and local media, further amplifying its reach into Maine households.

The DeepCwind initiative exemplifies the intricate nature inherent in many science marketing programs. Your marketing program is unique and shaped by your role, the product's stage of development, and the specific needs of the audience it must engage. The lessons from this initiative offer practical insights for anyone tasked with similar challenges, showcasing the importance of strategic thinking, stakeholder engagement, and adaptability in achieving success.

UNRAVELING MARKETING STRATEGY

Crafting a compelling and effective science marketing strategy involves an interplay between analysis and creativity.

ANALYTICAL APPROACH: THE SCIENCE OF MARKETING

The analytical approach acts as the backbone of strategy development. This component is all about objective assessment, data gathering, and logical thinking. Let's break down what it entails:

1. **Data gathering:** This involves extensive market research, surveys, and interviews to collect quantifiable information about the market, customer behavior, competitors, and other essential factors.

2. **Data analysis:** Here, the gathered data is dissected to unearth patterns, trends, and insights. Statistical methods and predictive modeling can help in understanding the target audience's preferences, identifying market opportunities, and forecasting potential challenges.

3. **Evidence-based decision-making:** This phase involves synthesizing all the analytical insights to formulate strategies. It's about aligning the product or service with the market demand, pricing, positioning, and promotional methods grounded in facts and evidence.

CREATIVE COMPONENT: THE ART OF RESONANCE

Contrasting the analytical method is the creative aspect of science marketing. This part is subjective and taps into human intuition, emotion, and aesthetic sensibility. Here's what it includes:

1. **Understanding emotions**: This is about delving into the psychological and emotional triggers of your target audience. What motivates them? What fears or concerns might they have? How does your product or service align with their values or aspirations?

> CRAFTING A COMPELLING AND EFFECTIVE SCIENCE MARKETING STRATEGY INVOLVES AN INTERPLAY BETWEEN ANALYSIS AND CREATIVITY.

2. **Storytelling and branding**: The creative process involves weaving a compelling story around your product or scientific innovation. It's not just about presenting facts but also connecting them with a narrative that resonates with your audience's beliefs, needs, and desires.

3. **Design and aesthetics**: From visual design to user experience, the creative component also encompasses the way the product is presented. It includes the design of marketing materials, website, packaging, and even the product itself, all aiming to appeal to the aesthetic sensibilities of the target market.

4. **Intuitive strategy development**: Sometimes, market insights may not be clear-cut, and data alone may not provide the full picture. Here, intuition, experience, and innovative thinking play a vital role in shaping a marketing strategy that aligns

with the unique dynamics of the scientific and technological landscape.

INTERPLAY BETWEEN ANALYSIS AND CREATIVITY: THE BALANCING ACT

The intersection between analytical rigor and creative intuition is where the most potent and effective marketing strategies emerge. However, finding the right balance between these two elements can be challenging.

Here are some examples of how they interact positively:

- **Informing creativity with analysis:** Analytical insights don't just guide strategic decision-making; they can also fuel creativity. Understanding the target audience, market trends, and competitive landscape helps in crafting messages, visuals, and experiences that resonate on a deeper level.
- **Enriching analysis with creativity:** Conversely, creative thinking can add nuance and depth to analytical processes. Sometimes, numbers and patterns don't tell the whole story. Creative interpretations and insights can uncover hidden opportunities or threats, offering a more comprehensive understanding of the market.

Challenges often arise that demand both analytical precision and creative ingenuity. One such challenge is the overreliance on data. While numbers and evidence are essential, focusing too much on them can lead to rigidity, missing the subtleties of human emotion and cultural nuances. The solution here is not to abandon data but to enrich it. By incorporating qualitative insights, empathetic understanding, and creative intuition, teams can utilize focus groups, interviews, and storytelling to gain a deeper understanding of customer emotions and values.

Another common and related obstacle is paralysis by analysis, where the pursuit of perfect data or overanalysis leads to delays and missed opportunities. Embracing the iterative nature of marketing can alleviate this issue. By starting with the best available data, applying creative thinking, launching, and then refining based on real-world feedback, teams can move forward without being bogged down.

Finally, the lack of integration between analytical and creative teams can lead to disjointed strategies. This challenge highlights the importance of collaboration and alignment within the organization. By fostering collaboration through regular cross-team meetings, shared goals, integrated project management, and encouraging teams to appreciate and leverage each other's strengths, an environment is created where both analysis and creativity can thrive.

Through a careful understanding of these challenges and the implementation of the mentioned solutions, you can craft strategies that align the logical with the imaginative, the factual with the emotional. You can connect with their highly educated and analytical audience on a level that transcends data, engaging both the mind and the heart.

ROBOCHIMERA'S STRATEGIC BALANCE

Imagine a fictional robotics company, RoboChimera, which stands at the forefront of technological innovation. They've created a cutting-edge robotic arm destined to reshape a specific manufacturing process, a brilliant fusion of engineering mastery and design elegance.

The analytical approach kicks in first. Initial market research suggests an aggressive market penetration strategy—swiftly introducing the product at a low price point to gain market share rapidly. Data shows a potential void in the market, and numbers crunch toward a quick launch. But the intricacies of the robotics market, steeped in tradition and often slow in adopting new technologies, raise a cautionary flag. A rushed approach could lead to skepticism and resistance, rather than the desired enthusiasm and mass adoption.

Enter the creative component. Intuitive insights reveal that the market's heart and soul might not be captured by numbers alone. There's a need for empathy, an understanding of the fears, aspirations, and values that resonate with potential customers.

So the strategy begins to evolve, informed by analysis but enriched by creativity. A slower, more considered product launch is planned, allowing for extensive demonstrations and trials. Marketing materials are thoughtfully designed, weaving a compelling story around Robo-Chimera's innovation that resonates with the audience's beliefs, needs, and desires. Every visual, every message, every experience is tuned to appeal to both the logical and emotional sensibilities of the target market.

Along the way, challenges arise. The tension between data-driven decision-making and creative intuition creates moments of uncertainty. There's a fear of overreliance on data, a concern of paralysis by analysis, a need to ensure that creativity is not disconnected from the market reality.

RoboChimera addresses these challenges by fostering collaboration between analytical and creative teams, encouraging cross-team dialogues, shared goals, and integrated project management. They embrace an iterative approach, starting with the best available data, applying creative thinking, launching, and refining based on real-world feedback.

The result is a marketing strategy that aligns logical thinking with imaginative intuition, factual evidence with emotional resonance. RoboChimera connects with its highly educated and analytical audience on a level that transcends mere data, engaging both the mind and the heart.

This example illustrates the robust collaboration between analytical insights and creative perspectives. This nuanced approach, where research and creativity come together to inform and enrich each other, may allow RoboChimera to navigate the robotics market successfully.

THE BACKGROUNDER

The success of any science marketing strategy hinges on the understanding of complex factors. Let's explore how to map out this understanding through the use of a backgrounder and marketing brief. As you read, consider how a detailed backgrounder could refine your current marketing approach.

Essentially, the backgrounder is a comprehensive document that captures vital information about the organization, its product, and the market landscape. It delves deeply into everything from product features, target audience, the unique value proposition, key personnel, and market dynamics. (These days, the backgrounder is usually less of a "document" than a resources folder with several subfolders.)

On the other hand, a "brief"—which we'll delve into a little later—is a document that derives from the information in the backgrounder. It synthesizes the information into a clear, concise guide that directs the marketing strategy and the execution of that strategy. It generally includes an overview of the organization and product, the marketing objectives of the specific campaign or activity you are briefing, the target audience, the key message(s), the strategy, and the specific tactics to be used.

Confused? Don't be. While both the backgrounder and the brief seem very similar, they serve different roles. The backgrounder is a comprehensive resource, while the brief is a focused guide for action based on that resource. Both are important in the overall marketing process, and writing them both well is crucial for a comprehensive marketing strategy. We'll go into the backgrounder first.

When creating a backgrounder, we spend hours gathering, sifting, sorting, and evaluating elements that may inform marketing goals and campaign strategy. The goal is to compile a comprehensive resource for your team so that they don't have to seek out this information every time they need it. It could be used by a media relations team to generate talking points in response to an important issue, by a content planner creating an editorial calendar for the organization's blog, or by the marketing strategist to determine which trade shows and conferences would be most relevant for the team to attend. As you learn more about the product or industry, this information can shift. The backgrounder, therefore, is actually a dynamic resource that evolves over time.

A comprehensive backgrounder should include the following:

- Audience identification and personas
- Value vows
- Marketing messages
- Brand story
- Founder's story
- Biographies of key personnel and their areas of expertise
- Organizational charts
- Detailed descriptions of products, including technical specifications, photography, and materials we can use as proof points (such as testimonials or relevant peer-reviewed research)
- Intellectual property portfolio
- Market research

This book is not intended to be a deep dive into market research. However, we should touch on a few standard models that we find useful in most cases with our clients at High Touch Group—in particular, the 5 Ps, SWOT analyses, and Porter's Five Forces—in addition to audience research (e.g., focus groups and experience surveys) and competitive analyses. These models synthesize and summarize the research from the backgrounder into useful components for marketing campaigns.

MARKETING'S FIVE PS

Understanding the core principles that guide your marketing efforts is vital. Enter the Five Ps of marketing: a straightforward yet often neglected concept that forms the basis for any successful strategy. Each *P* represents an essential component that must be carefully considered to craft a holistic approach.

- **Product:** In science-specific industries, "product" extends beyond physical goods to encompass scientific services, research value, or any solution meeting the specific needs of a target market. It must offer a unique solution or advantage over competitors, whether through technological innovation, scientific excellence, or user-centered design.
- **Price:** Setting the right price involves a fine balance between cost, market expectations, and perceived value. Novel products can present challenges in pricing, given the high costs of research, development, and market introduction. A carefully constructed pricing strategy considers these factors, aligning with both financial realities and market perceptions.
- **Place:** The "place" element is more than a physical location; it's the mechanism through which your product reaches the intended audience. Whether selling directly to research groups

or leveraging specialized distributors, the selected channels must ensure accessibility while complying with industry standards and regulations.

- **Promotion:** Effective promotion for scientific products often requires an educational approach, focusing on demonstrable efficacy and building trust. Techniques can vary from highlighting peer-reviewed publications to strategic content marketing, such as webinars or case studies. The key is to not only educate but persuade the audience to act, aligning with the broader objectives of your marketing campaign.

- **People:** Understanding the behavioral qualities of your target audience is fundamental. In scientific product sales, for instance, this could include researchers, scientists, IT professionals, or other influencers in the purchasing process. Customizing marketing strategies to these specific audiences ensures a tailored approach that resonates with their needs and preferences.

The Five Ps are more than independent variables; they are interconnected facets that collectively define your marketing approach. Ignoring any single *P* can lead to an unbalanced and ineffective strategy. For instance:

- Selling a product without proper price research might lead to misalignment with market expectations, reducing its appeal.
- Listing a product with a distributor without an accompanying promotional strategy could lead to underexposure and limited reach.
- Developing a product without a clear understanding of customer needs might result in a solution searching for a problem, rather than addressing a genuine market demand.

In essence, the Five Ps guide the development and execution of a comprehensive marketing strategy. By providing a broad yet incisive overview of the "marketing mix," they help bridge the gap between product and customer, ensuring that your potential customers know about the product, understand its value, and are motivated to purchase it.

By applying these principles with precision and awareness, science marketers can create robust, adaptable strategies that speak to the unique challenges and opportunities of their specific field.

SWOT

The SWOT analysis is a strategic planning tool used to identify an organization or product's *s*trengths, *w*eaknesses, *o*pportunities, and *t*hreats. It is an indispensable strategic tool for assessing the internal and external factors that influence an organization's competitive position. Careful application of this analysis reveals insights and opportunities that can shape the direction of marketing strategies in scientific industries.

- **Strengths:** Understanding the inherent advantages within your organization or product line is paramount. Your strengths may include technological superiority, proprietary processes, or a uniquely skilled team of engineers.
- **Weaknesses:** Recognizing the limitations of your organization or products allows for targeted improvements. Whether it's outdated technology, a narrow product range, or deficiencies in manufacturing capacity, identifying these areas opens avenues for growth and innovation.
- **Opportunities:** External market conditions often present untapped potential. Identifying opportunities in emerging

technologies, new market segments, or potential partnerships can help you stay ahead of the competition.

- **Threats:** External challenges can also pose significant risks. A changing regulatory environment, the introduction of competitive products, or fluctuations in funding and investment could threaten your position. Vigilance in recognizing and mitigating these threats is vital.

The integration of SWOT analysis into strategic marketing planning can guide informed decision-making, enabling alignment with long-term goals and adaptability to the rapid changes inherent in many marketplaces.

PORTER'S FIVE FORCES

Porter's Five Forces model provides a comprehensive framework for evaluating the competitive forces that shape an industry. Its application within the context of science marketing offers a nuanced understanding of the dynamic forces influencing success. This model can help you understand:

1. **Competitive rivalry:** Assessing the level of competition in your specific scientific niche is vital. The number of competitors, their capabilities, and the uniqueness of their offerings can significantly affect market dynamics. Staying informed of rival strategies can drive better positioning.

2. **Supplier power:** In specialized markets, suppliers may hold considerable influence. The availability of critical components or specialized materials could affect pricing, timelines, and manufacturing capabilities. Building strong relationships with suppliers and exploring alternatives can mitigate potential challenges.

3. **Buyer power:** Customers in science-driven industries often have specific needs and high expectations. Their power in influencing product specifications, pricing, or service levels cannot be underestimated. Understanding buyer behavior and adapting to their requirements ensure alignment with customer needs.

4. **Threat of substitution:** Emerging technologies and innovative solutions could replace established products. Keeping abreast of technological advancements and aligning with ongoing research and development efforts can minimize the risks associated with substitution.

5. **Threat of new entrants:** Barriers to entry, such as high investment costs or specialized knowledge, can protect a market segment. However, vigilance is needed to monitor potential new entrants that may disrupt established norms.

THE BUILDING BLOCKS OF A MARKETING STRATEGY

Creating an account backgrounder is a vital initial step in devising a marketing strategy. Though it may seem like a demanding task, this groundwork lays the foundation for insightful, targeted marketing. The information gathered informs every subsequent stage, making the effort more than worthwhile. Next, we'll use that information to develop your marketing strategy.

Science marketing does not always adhere to a fixed "strategic formula." However, it is built upon a set of core principles that guide the development of a unique and effective marketing strategy. The essence of a compelling strategy lies in its ability to consider the client's needs and target audience, as well as the broader landscape of the product, science, process, or technology in question. The key building blocks of a marketing strategy include setting goals, understanding the target market, and positioning the product or service, among others.

THE ESSENCE OF A COMPELLING STRATEGY LIES IN ITS ABILITY TO CONSIDER THE CLIENT'S NEEDS AND TARGET AUDIENCE, AS WELL AS THE BROADER LANDSCAPE OF THE PRODUCT, SCIENCE, PROCESS, OR TECHNOLOGY IN QUESTION.

The account backgrounder plays a crucial role here. It serves as the bedrock from which we construct our strategy. The rich repository of data and insights it houses drives the development of a strategy that aligns with the client's aspirations and resonates with the intended audience. It's a treasure trove of cues that help us determine our strategic direction and focus our marketing efforts. In other words, the backgrounder is an important resource for developing the strategy.

The key building blocks of an effective marketing strategy include the following:

- **Goals:** Goals are the North Star that guides any strategy. They describe what your marketing efforts hope to achieve, be it increased awareness of the value your product provides, determining product-market fit, driving product adoption, or expanding into new markets. Goals should be SMART—*s*pecific, *m*easurable, *a*chievable, *r*elevant, and *t*ime-bound—to ensure they're focused and achievable.

- **Target market (a.k.a. audience):** This building block involves dissecting the audience's demographics, psychographics, and behaviors. This knowledge shapes the marketing strategy and informs decisions on messaging, channels of communication, and even the nature of the product or service offering. Your audience may be divided into decision makers and influencers. If you are supporting product sales, know who makes the final "buy" decision and who influences it, and whether that's different from your product's end users. It often is.

- **Value vow:** Commonly referred to as the "value proposition," the value vow is the defining answer to "What's in it for me?" It differentiates a product or service from its competitors. This proposition should be clear, compelling, and backed by evidence.

- **Positioning:** Positioning defines how the product should be perceived in the minds of the customers and relative to the competitors. It's about distinguishing your offering from others in the market, highlighting the unique value vow that makes it the best choice for your target audience.

- **Marketing channels:** Depending on the product or service and the target audience, different marketing channels will be more or less effective. Choosing the right mix of channels— trade shows, email, podcasts, media, and so on—is crucial for reaching the audience and delivering the message effectively.

- **Marketing messages:** Crafting the right messages is all about communicating the product's value to the audience effectively. It should resonate with the audience, address their needs and aspirations, and convey the unique benefits of the product or service. Most complex products have multiple audiences, and your messaging needs to be adapted for each. For example, let's say you are commercializing software that you originally developed to run your own lab more efficiently. You may know how to persuade other researchers that your product will help them because you developed it for scientists like yourself. But you may also need to consider how to message your software product to IT departments, purchasing agents, and administrators who do not have the same appreciation for the laboratory management problems your product solves.

- **Tracking success and failure:** Based on your SMART goals, what metrics do you need to track to know if your strategy has succeeded or failed? Changes in polling data, sales revenue, or something else? What leading indicators can you track in real time to help you make decisions and adjust throughout the strategy's life cycle? This is your measurement strategy, and we'll discuss it further in chapter 7.

While every strategy is unique, these building blocks provide the framework for crafting a comprehensive and effective one. However, just as no two scientific discoveries are identical, no two marketing strategies should be the same. It's crucial to study the strategies of similar programs or products to understand their limitations and benefits, discern their differences, and assess their effectiveness so you can devise a plan that's right for your situation. This analysis can help avoid potentially costly mistakes.

A NOTE ABOUT ETHICS

Ethical considerations form an integral part of shaping a marketing strategy, especially in the sciences. Just as truth and integrity form the bedrock of every scientific discovery, marketing strategies must be imbued with the same. These ethical considerations serve as a strategic cornerstone, creating a foundation of trust and credibility that resonates with both clients and consumers. By aligning marketing practices with principles of honesty, integrity, respect, and transparency, organizations not only uphold the noble pursuit of truth intrinsic to science but also cultivate lasting relationships with their audiences. The positive implications of ethical marketing are multifaceted, enhancing brand loyalty, fostering long-term success, and contributing to a fairer and more conscientious environment for science communication.

Ethics, naturally, influence the goals of a marketing strategy. Objectives should be transparent, honest, and reflect the genuine value of the product or service being offered. They should not exploit the customers' lack of knowledge or create unrealistic expectations. The commercial side of our industries tends to be highly regulated, and our ethical oversight is important in safeguarding regulatory intent.

Similarly, ethical considerations play a significant role in understanding the target market and positioning the product. When analyzing the audience, it's important to respect privacy norms and consent, ensuring that any data used for marketing purposes is ethically obtained and used. In terms of positioning, the product should be presented honestly, without overstating capabilities or underrepresenting potential risks. The value vow must be an authentic representation of the product's value, not a hyperbolic or misleading claim.

Ethics also impact the selection of marketing channels and the crafting of messages. Channels should respect the audience's boundaries, and science marketers should avoid intrusive or potentially harassing methods. Crafting the message, meanwhile, should center around honesty and respect, and focus on providing useful information rather than manipulative persuasion.

Adherence to ethical principles is not merely a legal or moral obligation. It is a strategic imperative that fosters trust and enhances reputation for all stakeholders. Doing so not only boosts trust and reputation for their brands but also contributes to a fairer and more conscientious environment for all science communication. I think that's something we all want—as marketers, consumers, and humans alike.

FROM IDEAS TO ACTION: CRAFTING THE BRIEF

We're now going to create a brief (cue the confetti). What we'll do next is distill everything we've done to this point into a tool that's useful for all stakeholders. This concise document acts as a fundamental resource that informs everyone about the project's core elements. It acts as a blueprint for all marketing activities related to a specific campaign or project and is shared with all stakeholders to keep everyone on the same page. It's a vital step that translates the account backgrounder and marketing strategy into actionable pieces. In an ideal world, the backgrounder and brief should provide all the information your marketing team needs to execute a campaign. Remember that your backgrounder is your primary informational resource for documenting your strategy in your brief.

Here are the essential components you should include in your marketing brief:

1. **Objectives:** Begin by outlining the specific intentions of the marketing campaign. These should be clear, measurable, and aligned with the organization's overall goals. Remember SMART? Use SMART.

2. **Target audience:** Who is the campaign targeting? Define your target audience as accurately as possible, using the demographic, behavioral, and psychographic information gleaned from your account backgrounder and strategy. Include a discussion of any applicable audience segments and their specific motivations.

3. **Product or service overview:** Provide a detailed overview of the product or service being marketed. Include the value vow and key selling points, which are especially important in the science industry where features and benefits can be complex.

4. **Competitive analysis:** Summarize the competitive landscape, including strengths and weaknesses of competing products or services, and how the product or service you're marketing stands out.

5. **Positioning and messaging:** Define how the product or service should be perceived by the target audience and the key messages that will be used to achieve this positioning. If you have multiple audience segments, delineate each group's specific messaging here. This should align to your strategy we discussed earlier in this chapter.

6. **Marketing channels and tactics:** Outline the marketing channels (e.g., social media, email marketing, content marketing) and tactics—for example, search engine optimization (SEO) and pay per click (PPC)—to be used. These should be chosen based on their effectiveness in reaching the target audience.

7. **Timeline and milestones:** Establish a clear timeline for the campaign, including key milestones such as launch dates and evaluation periods.

8. **Budget:** Define the budget for the marketing campaign. Include a breakdown of how the budget will be allocated across the various channels and tactics.

Your marketing brief may need to accommodate certain industry-specific considerations. For instance, the brief may need to include a section that addresses regulatory or compliance issues, given the stringent regulations often present with many scientific products and services. Also, the technical complexity of science products may require a more in-depth explanation of the product or service and careful consideration of how best to communicate these complexities in a way that is understandable, engaging, and persuasive for the target audience.

If you're part of an internal marketing team, the responsibility for crafting the brief might fall on a department head or operations lead. If you're an outside consultant, it's likely all on you. The goal, however, remains the same: to ensure your team is prepared to engage with subsequent planning activities, which could include the project timeline, market research, and more.

My team often uses the "rule of three." This principle is based on research that shows that people best process and retain information presented in patterns or sets of three—the smallest number of elements needed to form a pattern. We use this rule of three to construct a concise business description for each unique client: "This is the company that provides [X] to [Y] for [Z result]." This description captures the key tangible aspects of the business—the products or services offered, their target audience, and their benefit.

We also review the company's mission statement, if one exists (many science start-ups and even some larger science organizations don't have one). The purpose of this isn't to incorporate it into outward-facing messaging necessarily but to gain deeper insight into the company's ethos and intent. A clear example might be a client that produces robotic beverage systems. Their mission statement may prioritize reducing environmental waste in the food and beverage industry—one of the most wasteful consumer sectors—rather than the efficient delivery of beverages. This would be highly valuable information for any marketing program!

Remember, the purpose of a brief is to provide a clear and comprehensive guide for your campaign, ensuring that all stakeholders are aligned and working toward the same goals.

CASE STUDY: A HYPOTHETICAL ASTEROID-LANDING EQUIPMENT MANUFACTURER

Consider a hypothetical company that developed an innovative product designed to support the landing of future mining vehicles on asteroids. Their challenge was to introduce this groundbreaking technology to an international market. The central problem they faced was effectively demonstrating the product's reliability and performance under extreme conditions to potential clients and stakeholders.

To begin, a comprehensive backgrounder was created. This document gathered crucial information about the company's organization, the novel product, its unique value vow, and its intended target audience. It also considered the brand's story, history, key personnel bios, and the company's position within the competitive landscape. During research for the backgrounder, it was noted that the product demonstrations at industry conferences and trade shows weren't reaching the necessary decision makers (e.g., space agency officials and private space exploration companies).

Strategy development followed, drawing upon insights from partnerships with other successful space-tech companies. From these collaborations, the marketing lead gathered valuable marketing strategies, an understanding of the product features that resonated with clients, and the key factors that drove sales conversations. It was discovered that a competitor had employed a unique approach of using virtual reality (VR) to simulate their technology in action. This immersive demonstration allowed the other company to showcase their product's capabilities in a compelling, accessible manner that went beyond traditional demonstrations.

With this successful approach in mind, the company's marketing team posed a critical question: "What's more important to potential clients in the global market? To see the product in action, or to understand its impact on asteroid mining operations?" This question was instrumental in guiding the strategic approach for the international market.

A detailed marketing brief was then crafted, which delineated clear objectives: to introduce the asteroid-landing technology to the international market and to effectively demonstrate its reliability and performance under extreme conditions. The target audience was well defined, considering the complex demographics in the global space-technology market. The unique selling points of the product, especially its robust design and reliability under extreme conditions, were emphasized. A competitive analysis helped understand how to position the product effectively.

In terms of messaging, the focus was on the reliability of the asteroid-landing technology and its potential to revolutionize asteroid mining operations. Marketing channels were chosen to be predominantly digital media with a strong emphasis on immersive technology such as VR to achieve a targeted reach over several stakeholder groups. Given the budget restrictions, a timeline and milestones were crafted with keen attention to efficient resource utilization.

Informed by the strategy and the particulars outlined in the brief, a VR-based product demonstration was developed. This demonstration emphasized the reliability and performance of the asteroid-landing technology in a simulated extreme environment. Not only was this campaign financially viable, but it also addressed the core interest of the potential clients—the product's reliability.

Faced with the challenge of introducing an innovative technology to a diverse and international market, the company meticulously gathered information to understand its position and audience. By embracing a strategic approach inspired by successful industry practices, such as the use of VR for immersive demonstration, the company was able to pinpoint and address the core interests of potential clients. This involved not just focusing on showcasing the product but emphasizing its impact on asteroid-mining operations as well. The process underscores the value of a comprehensive backgrounder, clear strategy, and detailed brief, aligned with a deep understanding of the market and its unique demands. Such a thoughtful approach can serve as a blueprint for marketing efforts, ensuring alignment with business objectives and maximizing the potential for success.

KEY TAKEAWAYS

1. The backgrounder serves as a fundamental resource in the marketing process, capturing critical information about the company, product or service, and market landscape. It is a comprehensive and dynamic collection of information that informs marketing strategies, evolving with the client's growth and success. The process of creating a backgrounder involves rigorous information gathering, analysis, and summary.

2. The core principles of a unique and effective marketing strategy include setting goals, understanding the target market, positioning the product or service, developing a unique value vow, selecting marketing channels, and crafting the message. These building blocks are informed by the backgrounder.

3. A marketing brief acts as a fundamental resource for the marketing team and other stakeholders who work together on a campaign. It distills the comprehensive information from the backgrounder and strategy into a concise, actionable guide. It outlines the campaign's objectives, target audience, product overview, competitive analysis, positioning and messaging, marketing channels and tactics, timeline and milestones, and budget.

4. When crafting a marketing brief, consider industry-specific elements, particularly in highly regulated markets.

BIG IDEAS: CREATIVITY AND THE CAMPAIGN DEVELOPMENT PROCESS

Some people get their best ideas in the shower. Others might have a eureka moment while running or during their commute. Personally, I find my most inventive ideas come in moments of solitude (for example, in a bath surrounded by stacks of notebooks and research clippings). Rarely do I start the ideation stage without some insights from these scribbles to seed the process.

Conversely, some members of my team resort to video game breaks in the middle of brainstorming sessions. This might seem like an odd strategy, but it allows for a mental reset and builds camaraderie—all integral components of the creative process.

One of my most challenging (yet creatively rewarding) projects occurred during my time as the senior manager of digital and strategic marketing at the Jackson Laboratory (JAX). A venerable institution, JAX is well known for its scientific rigor and unique offerings like genetically specialized mice and advanced research databases. Despite this, in the rapidly evolving research market, the institution's image had a perception of stodginess, which worked against them in marketing their products.

Every year, JAX conducted a stand-alone marketing campaign in the form of a wall calendar. The calendar was offered free to customers and stakeholders. This was more than a mere organizational tool; it was a lead generation and nurture campaign unto itself. That said, the calendar was a little dry. My team's challenge was to breathe new life into this traditional asset. The initial project came with its own set of challenges, from the constraint of a tight timeline to the void left by the jettisoning of the underlying creative concept that had made the calendar so popular.

Recognizing the task's potential, I pitched moving the creative ideation phase off-site. My team and I rented an Airbnb in Boston, canceled our meetings, and dedicated our energy to birthing fresh ideas. The result was a calendar populated with medical infographics and interactive, three-dimensional puzzle pieces that assembled into cell types. This first rendition was well received, but we knew we could push it even further.

As the next year's calendar project rolled around, we brought our A-game. This time we set up shop in another Airbnb in Boston, taking walks along the waterfront and soaking in museum tours when we weren't brainstorming. It was around this time that I was reading *The Amazing Adventures of Kavalier & Clay* by Michael Chabon, and one of our team members, a comic book enthusiast, helped catalyze an idea.

We decided to reframe Rosalyn Franklin, the unsung scientist who helped uncover the structure of DNA, as the leader of an imaginary "Guild of Amazing Scientists" battling personified diseases.

This concept turned the calendar into a series of comic book covers celebrating the achievements of underappreciated scientists and recent technological breakthroughs, like CRISPR. As part of our concept, we invented JAX Comics, a fictional publishing brand with a backstory to support the narrative.

This was the first idea that we were truly excited about. While our conference room brainstorming sessions back at the office had led to decent concepts, nothing had felt original or fun. It wasn't until we escaped the constraints of our usual workplace that we unearthed our motivation, passion, and creative energy to actualize an idea so big that it demanded a second printing. In the end, we distributed more calendars than ever. More importantly, it validated my belief in the power of environments to spur creativity and the necessity of a fresh approach when you're hitting a wall.

WHAT'S IN A CAMPAIGN?

Now that you've established the backgrounder, strategy, and brief, it's time to launch a campaign. A "campaign" refers to a coordinated series of marketing activities and tactics designed to achieve specific goals within a time frame. It's a strategic approach used to promote a product, service, brand, or message to a target audience.

This stage encompasses pulling various marketing levers—advertising, public relations (PR), social media, content creation, events, promotions, and more—to deliver a consistent, differentiated message and elicit the desired responses from your target audience.

A campaign is typically guided by a central theme or concept, which lends cohesion and interest to each asset. Each campaign ultimately prompts its target audience to take a specified action, such as purchase a product, subscribe to a service, or endorse a cause.

Campaigns often involve multiple touchpoints over a defined period, spanning weeks or even months. They may integrate various media channels—both online and offline—to effectively reach the target audience. Throughout the campaign's duration, marketers track performance metrics and adjust to optimize their outcomes and meet their objectives and to evolve dynamically as they are implemented.

CREATIVE IDEATION IN SCIENCE MARKETING

Creativity is important in science marketing. However, a campaign that doesn't resonate with its intended audience—no matter how creatively conceived—will struggle to generate traction and meet its objectives.

Unfortunately, there isn't a one-size-fits-all approach to generating great ideas. Each campaign requires its own blend of approaches customized to persuade a particular audience segment. Some campaigns might benefit from a more emotive, narrative-driven style that draws in the audience with a compelling story. Others may require a more data-driven, evidence-based approach, presenting hard facts and figures in a visually engaging way. The creative approach that's ultimately taken should reflect the nature of the product being marketed, the characteristics of the target audience, and the overall goals of the campaign.

Preparation forms the foundation upon which all creative endeavors stand. It's like laying the groundwork before erecting a building; the solid base ensures that all subsequent structures hold firm. In our case, the account backgrounder and the brief serve as this foundation, providing a comprehensive and cohesive base for your creative solutions. This base ensures that your creative ideas are

PREPARATION FORMS THE FOUNDATION UPON WHICH ALL CREATIVE ENDEAVORS STAND.

always informed and aligned with your client's needs, making your campaigns more effective.

A vital part of this preparation involves developing a profound understanding of both the product and its target audience. Just as a river can't flow without a source, creative ideas can't flow without this deep understanding. Bluntly, if you don't fully grasp the brand's values, the product's benefits, and the target audience's wants, your creative ideas will miss the mark.

In previous chapters, I've emphasized the importance of diving deep into your product, your target market, and your value vows. This deep understanding allows you to uncover insights that you or your competitors may have otherwise overlooked. To get to the heart of your target audience's real problem, you need to understand the product, the market, and the target customer deeply. By defining the problem accurately, you can craft a solution that resonates with the customer—showcasing exactly how your product can solve their problem. This level of understanding paves the way for creative ideation that hits the bullseye more often than not, producing campaigns that resonate, engage, and ultimately, persuade.

WHY DO I HAVE TO BE CREATIVE?

For anyone wrestling with self-doubt or questioning the need for creativity in communicating their scientific products or discoveries, understand that it's normal to feel this way. You're stepping into new territory, and that can be intimidating. However, if you find yourself wondering, "Why can't publication history alone convey the importance of my product?" here are a few considerations.

First, let's dispel the notion of "If you build it, they will come." If you've created a remarkable product but fail to communicate its value effectively, it could easily end up unnoticed no matter how spectacular it is. It could be lost to the depths of the internet or, even worse, gather dust in a distributor's warehouse. To give your product the recognition it deserves, you need to make sure its benefits resonate and remain in the minds of your target audience. That's where creativity comes in.

In today's crowded, distracting market, standing out from the crowd is essential. You're not only competing with direct competitors; you're vying for attention amid a myriad of distractions. Even if you have an audience for your webinar, they are still quite likely getting emails from colleagues, seeing ads from competitors, and being allured by social media. An innovative product needs to break through the noise, grab attention, and leave a lasting impression. Here, creativity becomes a tool to carve out a distinctive space for your product.

Third, creativity aids in effectively and efficiently delivering your message. Your publications are important parts of your marketing and communications strategies, yes, but they don't make for light reading and are probably not appropriate for each audience segment you need to reach. To capture and hold attention, you need to communicate your message in a way that is clear, concise, and engaging. Creative marketing can help distil complex concepts into digestible and memorable messages, ultimately accelerating the understanding and acceptance of your product.

Finally, creative marketing helps your product stick in people's minds long after the first encounter. Humans are naturally drawn to stories, emotions, and unique experiences. These elements, when incorporated into your marketing efforts, can demonstrably enhance recall and recognition. This is particularly critical in the science industry, where concepts can be complex and abstract. By infusing creativity into your marketing, you increase the chances of your product lingering in the minds of your audience, fostering brand loyalty, and driving long-term success.

CREATIVE KINDLING

With the backgrounder and the brief in hand, we launch into the creative ideation process by addressing basic (but crucial) questions: What are we aiming to achieve with this campaign? Who are we attempting to convince or influence? How does our product differ from competitors' offerings? What are the key messages we need to communicate? And, perhaps most importantly, what emotions or reactions do we want to elicit from our audience?

As we delve further into the creative ideation process, we should bear in mind some of the consumption models that anchor it. One such model, John Dewey's "Consumer Decision Process" (further discussed by George Belch and Michael Belch in their book *Advertising and Promotion: An Integrated Marketing Communications Perspective*) describes the following stages of consumer behavior:

- Problem recognition
- Information search
- Evaluation of alternatives
- Purchase decision
- Postpurchase behavior

This process is guided by various other psychological mechanisms such as motivation, perception, attitude formation, integration, and learning. The key here is understanding the consumer's journey and their cognitive process. What problem is your product solving? What is driving the consumer's motivation? By focusing on these aspects, you can home in on the issue that your client or product is trying to resolve and the motivation that spurs your customer to purchase it.

Keeping the details of this process in mind is important. However, even if you understand what you need to do and why, there will be moments when, despite your team's exhaustive understanding of the product, the "big creative idea" seems elusive. In such instances, it's essential to step back and let the information percolate. Let the inspiration seep in.

I like to call this stage "creative kindling." Various methods can help unlock you or your team's creative potential. When confronted with a dry spell of ideas, I might take the dogs for a walk, meditate, visit a museum, or go see a movie. I browse advertising annuals or immerse myself in the news. Often, turning my thoughts away from the problem at hand rekindles my creativity and gets me thinking laterally more effectively than fixating on it.

Data, while invaluable, can at times become overwhelming, leading to a state of analysis paralysis. This is when a fresh perspective or a different environment can prove crucial. To clear the mind, begin by disengaging from the account clutter—review the account backgrounder and briefs thoroughly, and then set them aside. But—and this is crucial—remain mentally active. Quiet the discord of chaotic thoughts and maintain a balanced state of relaxed engagement. You can do whatever you need to shake up your routine, but be sure to keep your task in mind.

AS A MARKETER, IT'S YOUR DUTY TO BE AWARE OF THE STRESSORS THAT HINDER CREATIVE THINKING AND TO PROMOTE A CONDUCIVE ENVIRONMENT FOR IDEATION, AND ULTIMATELY OVERCOME THEM.

Creatives, whether they're illustrators, art directors, writers, or another sort, typically have their own repertoire of techniques to rejuvenate their minds.

The key is to recognize when your brain is overwhelmed with data and give it the space to reset. As a marketer, it's your duty to be aware of the stressors that hinder creative thinking and to promote a conducive environment for ideation, and ultimately overcome them.

Nurturing creativity and ideation involves the element of spontaneity. Exceptional campaigns need a spark to kindle, fuel to sustain, and time to mature. It's often beneficial to host brainstorming sessions with the people entrusted to be creative on your behalf (and, if that person is you, yourself). You can role-play games involving the product or customer or even interchange roles. For instance, have designers write taglines while writers sketch concepts. Imagine your product as an animal or a superhero. What traits would it have? Remember, the most impactful idea rarely emerges at the beginning; it needs time, a nurturing environment, and a bit of serendipity.

PUTTING IT ALL TOGETHER: CREATING THE "BIG IDEA" CAMPAIGN

As you work to bridge the gap from creative ideation to campaign creation, the first critical step is to immerse yourself in the brief. Have I mentioned that already? The answer, of course, is "yes." That's because a thorough understanding of the brief provides the bedrock upon which your campaigns are built.

The culmination of all that creative brainwork lies in the formulation of a compelling "big idea." This is the supercool and compellingly creative "thing" that your campaign is built around. Here are a couple of real-world examples of effective campaigns:

- **"A Diamond Is Forever" (De Beers), 1947:** De Beers, a mining company that specialized in diamonds, launched a memorable marketing campaign with its slogan, "A Diamond

Is Forever." The campaign transformed the diamond market by associating diamonds with timeless love and commitment. Even today, more than seven decades later, this phrase remains synonymous with the brand.

- **"Intel Inside" (Intel), 1991:** Intel's famous campaign focused on promoting a computer component that consumers usually don't think about—the microprocessor. Paired with a distinctive jingle, this campaign set Intel apart as a leader in the tech industry and demonstrated the power of brand building in a business-to-business (B2B) context.

The "big idea"—the central concept—becomes the heart around which your campaign orbits. Here are some of the critical elements that your own campaign should include:

- **Name of the campaign:** Choose a name that embodies the spirit of your campaign and captures the attention of your target audience.
- **Campaign definition:** A one- to two-sentence definition that encapsulates the essence of your campaign.
- **Distinctive elements:** Create unique visual and/or written elements that make your campaign stand out. These could include white papers, walk-through videos, webinars, live demonstrations, advertisements, and other assets.
- **Strategy and tactics:** Develop a comprehensive strategy outlining your campaign objectives and develop your tactics to achieve them.
- **Audience and channels:** What are your audience segments? For example, are you targeting both end users of your product and purchasing agents? Which channels will reach your segments?

- **Value vow:** Define what makes your product or service unique. How does it solve a problem better than the competition?

- **Brand story:** Connect with your audience by crafting a compelling brand narrative that resonates and helps build a strong brand identity. How does this campaign fit into the overarching narrative of your brand?

- **Messaging and call to action (CTA):** Delineate your messaging by audience segment. Identify the action you want each segment to take after interacting with your campaign. Make it clear and compelling.

- **Budget:** Plan your budget meticulously to ensure optimal use of your resources without compromising on the campaign's effectiveness. You may need to adjust your channel strategy to meet budget constraints.

- **Campaign schedule:** Develop a comprehensive timeline that lays out the rollout of the campaign to ensure timely and smooth execution. Include relevant milestones.

- **Compliance and regulatory requirements:** Understand and incorporate the necessary regulatory requirements to ensure your campaign aligns with legal and ethical standards.

- **Mandatories:** This campaign may have certain "mandatories," such as firm launch deadlines, specific photography requirements, or nonstandard asset review procedures. Note the mandatories in this section and be sure to review them with your team.

Once your campaign is assembled, the subsequent question arises: How do you measure its effectiveness? We'll dive deeper into data gathering, analytics, and evaluating marketing effectiveness in a future chapter, but for now you should think about:

- **Establishing clear goals:** Define success for your campaign. This could range from heightened brand awareness to increased sales, improved website traffic, or higher levels of customer engagement.
- **Utilizing analytics tools:** Tools such as Google Analytics, social media analytics, and email marketing analytics offer valuable data on campaign performance.
- **Conducting A/B testing:** Test two variations of your campaign to determine which performs better. This could involve something as simple as a different headline or as extensive as a completely different visual design. This is an example of how many digital campaigns respond dynamically midstream to produce the most effective results.

Remember, data is your ally. It's not merely about constructing a creative campaign but about understanding its impact and making data-driven decisions to continuously improve your efforts. In the end, after all, science is all about hypothesizing, testing, and iterating based on results. Your marketing campaign should follow the same principles.

But that's all for later. Right now, you stand on the brink of bringing your campaign to life. It's time to step forward and execute your vision, armed with the knowledge and the tools to make your campaign a success.

CASE STUDY: A HYPOTHETICAL HIGH-TEMPERATURE SENSORS COMPANY

A European-based specialty sensor company found itself at an inflection point. Recognized for its robust suite of sensors designed for high-heat applications, the company confronted an issue: its products, indispensable to scientific research and industrial operations, were viewed as indistinguishable commodities, which limited their ability to increase sales. Easily substituted by rival offerings, their sensors were respected but not remarkable. The company understood that to amplify its market share, it had to boost the profile of its top-performing sensor brand, transforming it into an undeniable standout among its target audience.

The internal marketing lead summoned a team, and, collectively, they commenced formulating an inventive campaign. Their strategic advantage was the company's geographical closeness to top-tier raw material sources. The challenge lay in transforming an esoteric aspect of manufacturing into a compelling, unforgettable narrative for their scientific and industrial customers.

Their journey started by revisiting the mission and the brief—those pivotal documents we discussed earlier. Their brainstorming sessions focused on simple, yet profound questions: What are the campaign's goals? Whom are we striving to persuade or influence? They drilled further, tackling essential factors: How does our sensor stand apart from competitors? What are the crucial messages we must convey? And, perhaps most significantly, what emotional responses or reactions are we hoping to invoke in our audience?

The team centered their strategy on understanding the customer's journey and decision-making process. What problem did the company's sensor resolve? What fueled the customer's buying motives?

There were instances when, despite the team's comprehensive knowledge of their product, the "big idea" seemed unattainable. They shifted their attention from the issue, engaged in creativity-inducing activities, and cultivated a climate more conducive to ideation.

Eventually, the marketing team crafted a campaign centered around an animated mascot that symbolized the exacting nature of their manufacturing process and the resulting unyielding reliability of their sensors. This mascot, dubbed "Thermis," became an emblem of the company's dedication to high-quality raw materials and stringent manufacturing standards.

For disseminating their concept, they devised a multichannel marketing campaign. LinkedIn served as the primary platform due to its extensive B2B networking capabilities. Here, they published a series of animated videos and infographics featuring Thermis, showcasing the unique properties of their sensors and how they outperformed competitors.

For email marketing, they adopted a segmented approach, customizing messages for different customer profiles—researchers, aerospace professionals, and industrial operators. These emails included product fact sheets, user testimonials, and invitations to exclusive webinars.

They also hosted industry-specific webinars, spotlighting use cases of their sensors in various high-heat scenarios. These sessions, apart from providing a platform for detailed product discussions, allowed potential customers to interact directly with their team of engineers and product specialists.

Their diligent efforts bore fruit. Within just one year, the company experienced a 20 percent surge in sales and a 12 percent growth in market share, a noteworthy achievement in the specialty sensor manufacturing market. The campaign not only augmented its brand visibility but also strengthened its standing as a manufacturer that scientists and industrial professionals could trust for consistently top-quality sensors.

KEY TAKEAWAYS

1. A marketing campaign is a strategic, coordinated series of activities designed to achieve specific goals within a defined time frame.

2. Campaigns are steered by a central theme or concept—a "big idea"—that delivers a consistent, creative message across diverse marketing channels to provoke desired responses from the target audience.

3. The key to a successful science marketing campaign is marrying creativity with a deep, industry-specific understanding. This involves thorough preparation and comprehension of the client, brand, product or service, and target audience. It enables tailoring creative campaigns to effectively resonate with the audience and achieve campaign goals.

4. Embracing creativity in science marketing is essential. It shouldn't be intimidating. By leveraging creativity, we can break down complex scientific concepts, create compelling narratives, and ensure that our product or discovery captures attention, resonates with the audience, and leaves a lasting impression.

5. Measuring the campaign's effectiveness is as important as its creation, especially if you are from an external agency or will need to defend your campaign's results for some other reason, such as in a future budgeting cycle. This stage includes establishing clear goals, utilizing analytics tools, and conducting A/B testing and midstream campaign adjustments.

CHANNEL TACTICS FOR SCIENCE MARKETING

A few years ago, I found myself waking to another sweltering morning in Da Nang, Vietnam. Social media channels that usually buzzed with local news had more recently been filled with ominous reports of a new threat—COVID-19. My family had decided to stay in Vietnam even though the borders were closing, and so we were glued to our phones each day, watching for news from our new home and the US, where most of our family was. On this particular day, the media had a different tune—literally. Solemn updates about the spreading virus were interspersed with a catchy new jingle: *"Cùng rửa tay xoa, xoa, xoa, xoa đều ..."* (translation: "Together, wash your hands and rub, rub, rub evenly ...").

This wasn't your typical public service announcement. It was fun and engaging and had a great beat. A collaboration between Vietnamese musicians and the national health ministry, the music video had, by the time I came across it, already received millions of views on YouTube.

The song, titled "Ghen Co Vy," was based on the melody of a popular V-pop hit, "Ghen," reimagined by the originator, Khac Hung, in collaboration with Vietnamese health officials. It wasn't just an earworm—it conveyed a critical message about handwashing and sanitation, public health practices that were crucial to mitigating the spread of COVID-19. The magic of "Ghen Co Vy," however, extended past its catchy melody and lyrics. An energetic dancer named Quang Dang took it further, choreographing a vibrant dance that mimed proper handwashing techniques. The dance quickly evolved into the #ghencovychallenge on TikTok. People around the world followed his moves, thus spreading not just the dance but the song's message.

The campaign became a viral phenomenon. John Oliver, the host of *Last Week Tonight*, couldn't resist featuring it on his show, where he referred to it as a "genuine club banger." This exposure catapulted the PSA to international popularity, a rarity for any public health message—especially one from Vietnam.

Vietnam had done more than simply promote essential health guidelines to its citizens; public health agencies leveraged specific marketing channels to reach as much of the population as possible. If you lived in Vietnam at the time, you couldn't avoid seeing the video on television, Facebook, Twitter, TikTok, screens in airports and hospitals, and anywhere else. In doing so, Vietnam not only garnered respect on the global stage for its handling of the crisis but, importantly, persuaded the general population to take personal hygiene seriously—a cornerstone of effective COVID-19 mitigation in densely populated regions.

The Vietnamese example underscores the potential of clever marketing in public health contexts. By transforming an important message into a multimedia asset that resonated with the public, and by getting it to its target audience through a variety of channels,

Vietnamese health officials effectively communicated crucial information to a broad audience, particularly the youth who often struggle to access reliable information. It highlighted the vital role of awareness and information in empowering the public to combat the pandemic.

TUNING TO THE RIGHT CHANNELS

Up to now, we've mostly focused on planning and strategy—the essential groundwork for building effective marketing campaigns. A sturdy foundation in strategy helps to shape and guide your initiatives, ensuring they align with your core objectives. It enables you to define your target audience accurately, understand their needs, and develop relevant messaging. Your foundation enables you to design campaigns that resonate with your audience and inspire them to act. Moreover, it ensures your marketing resources—both time and money—are used effectively and efficiently, maximizing return on investment.

In this chapter, we'll delve into how to get your messages to your audience via marketing channels. You can think of a marketing channel like a television channel: it exists to serve specific content to a specific audience. Here are a few examples:

- LinkedIn is a social media channel that provides business professionals a space to network and share relevant content.
- Email newsletters provide a personalized channel to keep professionals, researchers, and interested parties updated.
- Scientific journals and magazines (e.g., *Nature, Advanced Materials, Science*) serve as respected channels for sharing research, product advertisements, and technical articles.

Below, we'll delve into an arsenal of marketing channels. Bear in mind that by the time you're reading this, the landscape may have shifted. Some new ones may have appeared, while others may have vanished, carried away by the ebbs and flows of funding and preference. Considering this, I'll strive to remain as general as possible without sacrificing practicality and applicability.

WEBSITES

You need a good website. Full stop. I'm astonished at the number of great science organizations that either do not have a website or the one they have looks like it was developed in 1998. It doesn't matter if your niece/brother-in-law/summer intern designed a website once—you need to entrust your website to a professional who is contractually obligated to provide you with good, objective service. At a bare minimum, your website needs to:

- Function as expected by users
- Communicate your value vow
- Feature clear CTAs with ways for your audience to actually take an action (e.g., contact you, place an order, follow your research)
- Be optimized for search (i.e., SEO)

YOUR WEBSITE IS YOUR BILLBOARD, YOUR BROCHURE, YOUR SALESPERSON, YOUR SUPPORT LINE, AND YOUR SOURCE OF TRUTH.

Your website is your billboard, your brochure, your salesperson, your support line, and your source of truth. It's not just a necessity—it's your global ambassador. Treat it with the importance it deserves by working with a thoughtful design and development resource. Once launched, don't neglect it—your website is your haven for news, events, links to publications, and more.

SOCIAL MEDIA

In today's digital marketing landscape, social media presents both opportunities and significant challenges for any science organization. As we saw with Vietnam's "Ghen Co Vy" handwashing campaign, social media can connect, engage, and build relationships on a global scale. It can take complex concepts and make them resonate with your audience, driving interest and positioning your company as an industry thought leader.

On the other hand, capitalizing on the potential of social media is far from simple. The social media environment is densely populated and volatile. Gaining visibility can be difficult and expensive. Even the concept of "virality" is nearly outdated amid the deluge of "viral" content that screams for attention. And while some social media platforms rise and flourish (think TikTok), they can also peak and fade in an instant. Remember Friendster? How about Vine? Google+? Orkut? Peach?

For science marketers, the challenges are even more pronounced. Converting the intricacy and specialization of products, services, or research into engaging, easily digestible content for a B2B (business-to-business) or B2C (business-to-consumer) audience requires a fine balance and considerable skill. It's akin to transforming a public health message into a catchy song and dance.

Despite these hurdles, social media is a viable channel in a science marketer's arsenal. The important thing is this: *it can't be done half-heartedly*. Don't just do it because it's low-hanging fruit and "you're supposed to." Success in social media requires more than a sporadic presence; it necessitates an energetic commitment to ongoing engagement. This entails a demanding cadence of regularly scheduled posts, active responses, and continual content generation. High-quality images and videos and a clear, consistent message are key. Ask yourself:

"Do I have the time to do it right?" If the answer is *yes*, then ask yourself: "Does my organization have enough compelling, professional imagery, video, and news to post something new ten to fifteen times a week?" If the answer is *no*, certain social media channels might not be worth your time investment (at least for now).

However, if you discover that you are, indeed, ready to move ahead with social media—congratulations! Let's move on. To leverage social media effectively, adopt the same strategic storytelling used in the "Ghen Co Vy" campaign. Break down your narratives into relatable stories that resonate with audiences. Utilize visually compelling formats such as infographics or videos to explain complex concepts. Engage your audience through interactive content such as polls or quizzes and consider partnerships with influencers to broaden your reach and credibility (more on this later).

Consider the following for a more effective social media strategy:

- **Strategic storytelling:** Break down your scientific narratives into relatable stories that resonate with audiences.
- **Visual appeal:** Use visually compelling formats such as infographics or videos to explain complex concepts.
- **Interactivity:** Engage your audience through interactive content such as polls or quizzes.
- **Influencer partnerships:** Consider collaborations with influencers to expand your reach and credibility.
- **Alignment with brand strategy:** Ensure your social media messaging is consistent with your broader brand strategy.

PODCASTS

Podcasts are effective channels for marketing science products and services, opening avenues for detailed discussion, expert insights, and personalized storytelling. Their long-form content format is ideal for breaking down complex scientific concepts, providing a platform where you can share your expertise and discuss your products or services in depth. They also build credibility and trust, which is invaluable in a context where accuracy and expertise are important.

Getting started with podcasts and interviews requires some preparation. Initially, it involves identifying relevant industry podcasts that align with your field and target audience. Once you have a list, reach out to the podcast hosts or producers and propose topics that would be of interest to their listeners. Podcast hosts and producers want to add value for their listeners (and their advertisers), so pitch topics where your expertise can genuinely contribute to the conversation.

To leverage podcasts and interviews most effectively, consider the following pointers:

- **Understand the audience:** Every podcast has its unique audience. Tailor your content and presentation style to match the listeners' expectations and interests.
- **Deliver value:** Ensure that your discussion adds something to the conversation—unique insights, industry trends, or actionable tips related to your field.
- **Promote ahead:** Amplify the reach of your podcast appearance by promoting it through your existing marketing channels.
- **Be authentic:** Authenticity resonates with listeners. Share your passion for your field, your successes, and even your failures. It builds relatability and trust.

Science marketers could face certain challenges with this channel (and, for that matter, nearly every channel we discuss in this chapter). One of the most common is effectively communicating complex scientific concepts in an understandable and engaging manner. Remember, the goal is to educate and engage your audience, not overwhelm them with technical jargon. A delicate balance between scientific accuracy and comprehensibility is crucial.

TRADITIONAL MEDIA

Traditional media—those on TV, the radio, or in print publications—provide a unique opportunity to market your product or research. Given the public's inherent trust in traditional media outlets, gaining coverage can significantly enhance your brand's reputation. And while these channels have seen audiences wane as digital options take center stage, they retain a sizeable influence (particularly among an older, more established generation).

To start with, identify journalists and reporters who cover science-related topics. Construct a compelling pitch that highlights the newsworthiness of your product or service. However, be cognizant of a significant barrier: capturing media attention. In an environment saturated with potential stories, getting the attention of editors, gatekeepers, and decision makers can be challenging, even for seasoned marketing professionals. As a novice in marketing, this barrier can seem even more daunting. However, ensuring that your pitch is timely, relevant, and engaging can significantly improve your chances of breaking through.

Here are some strategies to leverage traditional media interviews most effectively:

- **Prepare key messages:** Identify three to four key messages about your product or service. Use these as the core of your communication throughout the interview.
- **Timeliness:** Align your pitches with current news trends to increase relevance.

- **Follow-ups:** A courteous follow-up can keep your pitch top of mind for a journalist or reporter.

ACADEMIC JOURNALS

Securing publication in an academic journal is more than a seal of scholarly validation for your research; it serves as a direct communication tool to fellow professionals in the field, conveying the quality and novelty of your scientific findings. More than that, however, academic publication offers an added dimension to your marketing efforts. You can communicate your published research via your marketing channels to provide a base of "social proof" that bolsters the legitimacy of your offerings, not just to your scientific peers but also to a wider audience that includes potential customers, investors, and other stakeholders.

Despite its advantages, academic publishing also presents some challenges for science marketers. For example, the publication process is often lengthy and rigorous, which might not align well with the faster timelines of product development and marketing.

Let's say that you've received the great news that your manuscript has been accepted for publication. To leverage academic journals most effectively in your marketing strategy, consider these steps:

- **Reach out to your network:** Use your publication as a springboard for discussion with colleagues, with industry peers, and on professional networking sites such as LinkedIn.
- **Publicize your publication:** Highlight the publication on your website and share snippets or key findings on your social media channels, translating the science into digestible content for a nonspecialist audience.

- **Leverage the journal's reputation**: Incorporate mentions of the journal publication in your marketing materials, pitch decks, and investor communications to bolster your credibility.

PAID MEDIA

Paid media (a.k.a. "advertising that you pay for") is an important tool in the science marketing mix. The key advantage of paid media is its potential for precision. By investing in specific platforms, you're basically buying a ticket to put your message directly in front of a particular audience. Whether it's the readers of CompositesWorld magazine, subscribers to the Big4Bio newsletter, or fans of a niche scientific blog or podcast, the precise targeting potential of paid media can be instrumental in reaching your desired customer base.

> **BY INVESTING IN SPECIFIC PLATFORMS, YOU'RE BASICALLY BUYING A TICKET TO PUT YOUR MESSAGE DIRECTLY IN FRONT OF A PARTICULAR AUDIENCE.**

The first step is to identify your target market, where they spend their time, and what kind of messaging resonates with them. Explore potential advertising platforms that align with these insights. Be aware that start-up costs could be high, depending on the reach and effectiveness of the platform. Moreover, creating high-quality, engaging ads that convey your scientific message effectively could require professional creative resources.

To leverage paid media effectively, consider the following:

- **Optimize ad placement:** Choose platforms that align with your target audience's habits and preferences. Many publications will share "advertising kits" that outline their readership demographics, digital ad performance metrics, and such.

- **Invest in quality:** Make sure your ads are professionally designed and articulate your message effectively.
- **Track metrics:** Regularly monitor and analyze the performance of your ads. Adjust your approach based on what's working and what's not.

EARNED MEDIA

Earned media is the hoped-for result of many PR campaigns. It essentially represents the coverage you "earn" from external entities such as reporters, bloggers, or industry influencers based on the newsworthiness of your content. Contrary to a common misconception, these people are not "gatekeepers" who arbitrarily decide your fate from the top of a media mountain. In fact, they're often in a perpetual search for compelling and valuable content to present to their readership. It's your job to give it to them.

Embarking on an earned media strategy involves developing and distributing high-quality, relevant content. You need to create compelling narratives around your product or service that can capture the interest of these media professionals. A good place to start is by drafting and disseminating press releases about new research findings, product launches, or company milestones. Keep in mind that this approach is not without its challenges. Building relationships with media professionals takes time, and there's no guarantee your content will even be picked up for coverage.

One particular mistake that I see time and time again bears mentioning: not everything is newsworthy, or even appealing. Your new ISO certification is exciting to you, sure. It's not exciting to most of the world. I'd venture to say it's not even exciting to a lot of people in your own organization (I'm sorry to burst your bubble). Therefore, only the most focused industry publications may run the news. Same with your new website—I know that a new site is very exciting. It may be the first time you've had one. But to the world at large—a world in which websites are extremely common—it's not notable; therefore, an editor is not going to publish the press release that heralds its arrival. A good rule of thumb to consider is this: is the news first, last, new, or different? I don't mean in the context of your organization—I mean in the eyes of your audience. If it's not, then perhaps your energy is better spent creating content for your shiny new website and leveraging that tool instead.

To make the most of earned media, consider these pointers:

- **Build relationships:** Form strong connections with key media personnel in your industry. Offer regular, valuable insights to keep your brand top of mind.
- **Present well-packaged stories:** Ensure your content is easily digestible and compelling. Remember, reporters and bloggers are looking for stories that engage their audience.
- **Timely and relevant:** Keep abreast of current industry trends and hot topics. Tailor your content and pitches to fit within these narratives.

A NOTE ON CRISIS COMMUNICATIONS

Given the complexities of scientific fields, controversies, crises, or misinformation can and do emerge. When it happens, swift and organized communication responses are important.

Consider the case of SpaceX after the Falcon 9 rocket explosion in 2016. The incident occurred during a routine preflight test, resulting in the destruction of the rocket and a valuable satellite payload.

SpaceX's response was a model of effective crisis communication. Immediately following the incident, CEO Elon Musk took to social media to acknowledge what had happened and assure the public that a thorough investigation would be conducted. The company coordinated with regulatory authorities and provided regular updates on the investigation's progress, sharing findings and implementing changes to prevent future occurrences. Transparency, speed, and consistency were the hallmarks of their communication strategy.

This real-world example illustrates the importance of having a contingency plan in place. When confronted with a crisis, being prepared with well-thought-out responses can help manage the situation effectively, preserve your organization's reputation, and uphold public trust.

Consider these pointers when handling crisis communications:

- **Transparency is paramount:** Admit mistakes when they occur and share your plans to rectify them.
- **Speed and clarity:** Address crises promptly and ensure your messaging is clear and free of jargon.

- **Stay consistent:** Consistent messaging across all communication channels reaffirms your credibility.
- **Engage with media:** Leverage your relationships with media professionals to convey your side of the story.

WEBINARS

Webinars are an effective way to showcase the depth and complexity of a science product or service. With webinars, science marketers can delve into the intricacies of their offerings, underscoring their products' or services' unique advantages and potential applications in real-world scenarios.

By nature, webinars are interactive. They provide the opportunity to connect directly with potential customers or partners, foster an exchange of ideas, and open the floor to feedback or questions. This engagement can facilitate a deeper understanding of the product or service, not to mention a greater connection.

Starting a webinar does require some investment, mainly in terms of time and resources. In the initial phase, you need to identify a suitable platform to host the event (e.g., Zoom, Webex). These platforms offer features including screen sharing, live chat, and recording capabilities, but their use may come with subscription costs. Additionally, the development of high-quality scripts, presentations, graphics, and other content can also require a time or monetary investment.

To effectively leverage webinars, keep these pointers in mind:

- **Relevant and engaging content:** Since these platforms enable you to delve into the depth and complexity of your science product or service, ensure that the content you present is rich, engaging, and valuable to your audience. Make it as interactive as possible to foster engagement.

- **Promotion:** To attract attendees, you must promote your webinars or seminars through multiple channels—social media, email newsletters, or even paid advertisements.
- **Follow-up:** After the event, follow up with participants. You might share a recording of the event, share key takeaways, or extend an invitation for a one-on-one conversation to further discuss their interests or concerns.

"But what if no one comes?" It's a question I hear often, and it's a valid one. Sometimes, webinar attendance is so low that you wonder why you bothered at all. In the end, we can't control webinar attendance. We can, however, take steps to promote its success. One way is by creating compelling invitations that convey the value attendees will gain and ensuring the topic is one that will resonate with your target audience. If attendance is still low, all is not lost. Many webinars find "second lives" as follow-on marketing tools: gate your on-demand webinar and use it as a lead-gen tool, add it to a toolkit of resources when onboarding new customers, cut it up for social channels, and more. Remember, webinars are about more than just broadcasting information; they are an opportunity to engage directly with your target audience, build relationships, and position your organization as a thought leader.

WHITE PAPERS

These detailed guides or reports elucidate the science behind a product or service, revealing the unique benefits and innovative aspects that set your offering apart. They can be used to establish your organization as a thought leader in the industry. In addition, white papers can serve as a powerful lead generation tool. Potential clients that engage with white papers often demonstrate a level of interest and understanding that's indicative of their potential value as future clients or collaborators.

Starting with white papers requires an investment in both time and expertise. The process begins with the identification of a relevant topic that aligns with your product or service and is of interest to your target audience. A team of technical experts and writers then needs to collaborate to produce content that is accurate, insightful, and readable. Remember, the ultimate goal of a white paper is not only to inform but also to persuade the reader of the value of your product or service.

When leveraging white papers, consider the following points:

- **Quality over quantity:** Invest time in producing well-researched, well-written white papers. High-quality content can establish your organization's credibility and draw in a higher level of reader engagement.
- **Targeted promotion:** Plan your white paper's dissemination carefully. Use your company's social media channels, email newsletters, and even paid promotion to reach a targeted audience. Remember, a white paper's impact is determined not just by the quality of its content but also by how effectively it reaches potential clients.
- **Encourage action:** Include a call to action in your white paper. Invite readers to engage further with your organization, perhaps by scheduling a consultation or signing up for your newsletter.

EMAIL MARKETING

In a world saturated with apps and other digital tools designed for up-to-the-second connectivity, email can seem like a relic. The fact is direct email marketing remains a relevant and effective tool. When done right, it delivers your message straight into an environment that the recipient checks regularly. It's especially useful when paired with a curated list of relevant contacts, be it from industry events, your website, or other channels. It's cost-effective and offers a degree of customization and segmentation that few other channels can provide. For example, you can tailor your messages based on the recipient's previous interactions with your company, their interests, or their role within their organization, which can increase the impact of your efforts.

Getting started with direct email marketing does require some planning and foresight. It's essential to ensure you have permission to contact the individuals on your list—unsolicited emails can damage your reputation and violate regulations such as the General Data Protective Regulation (GDPR). Moreover, your email content must be engaging and offer value to prevent your messages from being labeled as spam.

Here are some pointers to effectively leverage direct email marketing:

- **Personalization:** Use the data you have about your contacts to personalize your emails. This could include addressing the recipient by name or referencing their specific interests or previous interactions with your company.
- **Value:** Ensure every email offers value, whether that's informative content, an exclusive offer, or a relevant update about your products or research.

- **Clear CTA:** Each email should guide readers to *do something*, such as meet with you at an event, download a white paper, or buy your product.

INDUSTRY INFLUENCERS

Influencers, with their established following and reputation, can extend your reach and lend credibility to your offerings in ways that traditional marketing channels might not. In the context of science marketing, the term "influencers" does not refer to burgeoning social media stars testing new cosmetic products or experiencing boutique hotels in far-flung locations. Rather, we're talking about building partnerships with leading scientists, respected researchers, or other notable professionals who are willing to espouse your cause (or even partner with it).

This strategy is powerful in the sciences, where trusted voices matter. Having an influential researcher or organization endorse your product or service can not only broaden your reach but also enhance your brand's credibility. They speak the language of your target audience and understand its needs, pain points, and aspirations, making their endorsements particularly impactful.

To start, identify potential influencers who align with your brand's values and have the right audience demographics. Reach out to them with a clear proposal that details the potential benefits for both parties. (You should also be ready for financial or other material considerations, as influencer partnerships often involve a form of compensation.)

Here are some tips on how to leverage influencer partnerships most effectively:

- **Clear messaging:** Ensure the influencer understands your product or service thoroughly so that they can communicate its benefits effectively to their audience.
- **Authenticity:** Choose influencers whose professional ethos aligns with your brand. Forced or misaligned partnerships can do more harm than good.
- **Engagement over size:** Don't simply consider the size of an influencer's following. An influencer with a smaller but highly engaged audience can often yield better results.

INDUSTRY-SPECIFIC ONLINE FORUMS/COMMUNITIES

Industry-specific online forums and communities are important channels for science marketing. These digital spaces provide unprecedented access to a concentrated community of professionals and users with shared interests and pursuits, making them prime marketing territories.

To leverage these forums, start by identifying the platforms most relevant to your field, such as ResearchGate, academic.edu, LinkedIn groups, or other specialized forums. Gaining credibility within these communities requires authentic and valuable contributions, rather than overt selling.

Here are some considerations for using these platforms effectively:

- **Authentic engagement:** Engage in ongoing discussions, ask insightful questions, and provide valuable inputs. The objective is to add value, not to promote your product or service directly.
- **Consistency:** Regular, meaningful engagement builds your presence and credibility within the community.

- **Share relevant content:** Share content such as research papers or blog posts that provide deeper insights into the discussed topics, while avoiding overt self-promotion.

TECHNICAL DEMONSTRATIONS

Technical demonstrations, whether via video or in person, are a powerful tool for marketing science products and services. They offer an unmatched opportunity to dissect the technical prowess of your product, explain its benefits, and connect it to the needs of your audience.

Planning an effective demonstration requires understanding your audience's familiarity with your product or service and tailoring the complexity of the demo accordingly. A demo aimed at industry peers could dive deep into the intricacies of the technology, while one for non-scientific stakeholders should focus on the tangible benefits delivered.

Here are key considerations for leveraging technical demonstrations:

- **Clarity and engagement:** Ensure your demo is clear, concise, and compelling. Use visual aids, analogies, and storytelling to make the information more digestible and engaging.
- **Interactivity:** Encourage audience participation by allowing for questions and real-time feedback during the demonstration.
- **Focus on the problem and solution:** Emphasize the issues your product or service resolves and how it stands out from alternative solutions.

EVENTS AND TRADE SHOWS

Trade shows play an indispensable role in science marketing. Though we'll delve more deeply into this channel in the next chapter, it's worth emphasizing the unique position these events hold for science marketers. Unlike many other marketing avenues, trade shows provide a tangible, face-to-face interaction platform that's crucial for the intricate nature of scientific products.

At their core, trade shows offer unparalleled opportunities to:

- Showcase and demonstrate complex products in a hands-on setting
- Engage directly with an array of stakeholders, from potential customers and funders to competitors and vendors
- Gather real-time feedback and insights to shape marketing strategies and product development

While trade shows come with many benefits, they can be resource intensive in terms of time, money, and labor. Success often hinges on meticulous planning and effective follow-up. Missing out on either can turn a potential opportunity into a missed one.

Here are some tips on how to leverage trade shows and events:

- **Plan early:** Ensure all logistical details, from booth design to lead collection, are sorted well in advance.
- **Engage actively:** Utilize the event to not just showcase but also network, learn, and collaborate.
- **Follow up:** Post-event communication with leads and contacts is crucial. It's where many actual deals start taking shape.
- **Stay updated:** Use the event to understand industry trends and adapt your marketing strategies accordingly.

TUNING TO THE RIGHT CHANNELS

Choosing the right marketing channels for your campaigns is both an art and a science. While the abundance of options might seem overwhelming, the key is to identify the platforms that will best resonate with your target audience and your brand message.

As you gain experience, the channel-selection process will become more intuitive and you'll be able to rapidly estimate your budget by channel based on audience size and past successes or failures. Although new events or publications might emerge, some foundational questions can guide your initial decisions.

- **What is your campaign goal?** If it is about driving product sales, how and where do your customers buy from you? Your marketing channels may be different for driving sales through (a) distributors, (b) your own online storefront, or (c) a sales team.
- **Where is your target audience?** They might read specific publications or attend certain events year after year. Prioritize channels where your audience already is instead of assuming that you will have the resources to bring your audience to you.
- **What is your budget?** This is crucial. If you are working with a limited budget, you should extend funds only when the return on investment (ROI) is a lower risk. For example, if you are an exceptionally good networker, it may make sense for you to attend events. If you are shy, maybe spend that budget elsewhere (or send a social butterfly).
- **What channels do you already own that may be appropriate for this campaign?** For example, your website and your organization's LinkedIn page are owned channels. Conversely, unless you are Jeff Bezos, the *Washington Post* is not an owned channel.

KEY TAKEAWAYS

1. In marketing, success stems not from a universal solution but from strategic planning, defining clear objectives and adopting a bespoke blend of tactics that effectively reach your target audience.

2. In a fast-paced, evolving digital landscape, the enduring power of innovative and creative communication cannot be overstated. Transforming a vital message into an engaging and shareable medium can effectively foster connections and inspire action, reinforcing the importance of creativity in science marketing.

3. Your website is not just a digital necessity but also your organization's ambassador to your target audience. It encapsulates your value vow and communicates it to the world. Ensuring it is functional, modern, error-free, and optimized and features clear CTAs is critical. Engaging professional services to create and maintain it is an important component of your marketing plan.

4. Select your channels wisely. You don't need to be everywhere all at once. Think about where your audience is most engaged and start there.

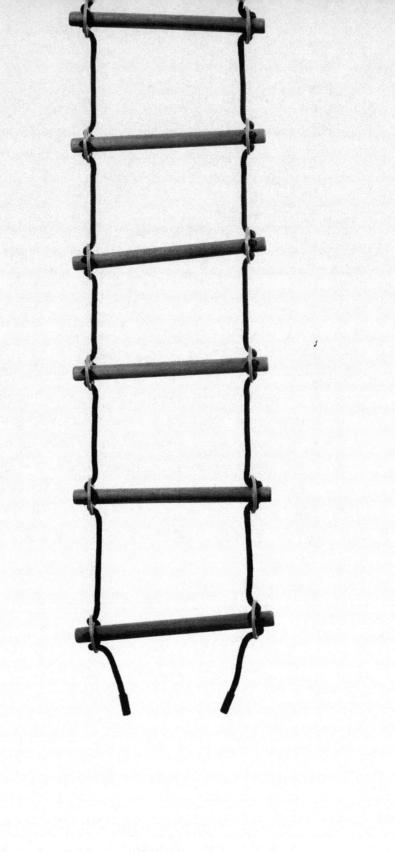

FROM EXHIBIT HALLS TO PODIUMS: NAVIGATING TRADE SHOWS AND PUBLIC SPEAKING

Trade shows offer a prime opportunity for networking, knowledge sharing, and showcasing research, products, and services. Virtual meetings serve a purpose, but few opportunities achieve these objectives better than a well-executed trade show campaign.

Trade shows are fundamental to most industries, which is why they deserve their own chapter in this book. One of the major benefits is the opportunity they provide to showcase your research or products in a focused setting. Given the inherent complexity of many of these topics, there's an undeniable advantage in being able to explain and demonstrate in person. Marketers can use trade shows as a platform to illustrate how a product functions and solves customers' problems while simultaneously highlighting any novel or distinctive selling points that set their product apart.

These events serve as crucial networking hubs. By bringing together industry professionals, academic and nonprofit researchers, funding agencies, and investors, large trade shows can facilitate direct engagement with your target audience. A single show may allow you to reach your potential customers, vendors, and funders all in one convention center. Your team can answer queries, receive immediate product feedback, solicit and nurture business deals, and even discover new avenues for collaboration with others in your field.

Importantly, trade shows are valuable occasions for creating opportunities for your sales team (or nearest equivalent) to generate sales in your booth, in a customer's booth, or at an after-hours event—perhaps one you host. The cleverer you are in developing and executing a trade show marketing strategy, the more likely you are to make those connections happen.

Finally, trade shows are a treasure trove of industry insight. By attending these events, science marketers can stay updated with the latest research, trends, innovations, and challenges. They help you identify and keep tabs on your competitors. This not only allows marketers to shape their strategies but also helps identify growth opportunities and maintain a competitive edge.

Having planned and participated in a significant number of events, I've developed an understanding of the nuances involved in the successful use of trade shows as a marketing channel and tool. There are a multitude of ways to participate in trade shows. This chapter walks you through the most popular options.

WALKING A TRADE SHOW FLOOR

It's nearly here: the date of your industry's premier trade show. Rather than elect for a booth of its own, your organization has decided to send you to walk the floor. Your tickets are booked. The exhibit floor is bursting with diverse, exciting exhibits. It's like a vacation! All you need to do is show up and let the experience wash over you.

Sorry, but I'm going to burst your bubble. If you want to extract any value from a trade show, it's not all about watching cool demos and finding free happy hours. To get your money's worth (or your organization's), more initiative is required. Your strategy starts with preparation before you even arrive.

First, be clear about your goals for this show. Are you there to get customers, find collaborators, or identify component vendors? Review the exhibitor list well in advance and identify which exhibitors align with your needs. For anyone important, find their email or connect with them on LinkedIn to request a meeting in advance. Reconfirm the meeting date, time, and location with them ahead of the show and make sure that you have everyone's cell numbers. For anyone you didn't get a chance to connect with before the show, mark their booth on your expo floor map. A clear game plan will guide your time and interactions during the show. Plan your route through the floor each day based on the following:

SUCCESSFUL TRADE SHOW ATTENDEES—THE ONES WHO GET THE MOST VALUE FROM THEIR TIME ON THE FLOOR—ARE THE ONES WHO TRY TO CREATE AND NURTURE CONNECTIONS.

- Your scheduled meetings
- Any talks, poster sessions, scheduled demonstrations, or networking events you want to attend while there
- The booths for organizations that you couldn't preschedule meetings with

Networking at these shows is critical to your success. Successful trade show attendees—the ones who get the most value from their time on the floor—are the ones who try to create and nurture connections. Here are a few tips to make the most of your time there:

- Use LinkedIn and other social media platforms to your advantage by following the trade show's hashtag. You can use hashtags to find and connect with other attendees ahead of time, identify networking events or presentations, and see what your customers, vendors, and competitors are talking about.

- Seek out relevant networking events. These are usually after-hours events hosting in booths or off-site at nearby hotels, restaurants, and bars. If you want to attend one that isn't open to the general audience, see if you have a connection that could get you on the guest list.

- Memorize a natural sounding "elevator pitch" about your organization, research, or product. Also develop a quick introduction to who you are and why you are attending the show. Practice these out loud in front of a mirror to make them sound natural and boost your confidence.

- If you, like me, are a bit awkward at a large gathering, I'll give you the advice that helped me the most: people like talking about themselves. Make a list of open-ended questions that you can ask to make conversation. Have a few test conversations like this to work out which questions work well and feel natural, and it gets much easier. Above all, be genuine and show interest in others, and you'll leave a lasting impression.

- Schedule time for self-care before, during, and after these events. Many of my colleagues wake up early for a run each day. For me, self-care means getting time with family and my dogs before and after I travel and making sure that I get enough rest each evening of the show.

- Trade shows are an endurance sport, and the right footwear is critical. Ensure that you wear shoes that can support this task. I own a lovely collection of shoes that I affectionately call my "sitting shoes" due to their heel height. They can transform a mediocre outfit into an outstanding one, but they never attend trade shows with me. Kitten heels and cute flats are your friends, ladies. Men's shoes can be almost as painful—gel inserts are your friends. In any case, bring backup shoes in case your original choice doesn't work.

- The rest of your wardrobe is important too. Know what's appropriate for this show. For example, an agriculture show might be more of a "plaid and jeans" event than your average oncology seminar. Try on your outfits before you leave your house to make sure everything fits well, check them for stains, and remove tags on anything new. Pack at least one extra outfit in case you spill coffee all over one. Leave enough time each evening or morning to iron.

- Your experiences may differ, but in cases where allergies, sleep issues, and the prospect of socializing with the sales team (and potential hangovers) are concerns, make sure to include your customized pharmacy essentials. I pack bandages and antibacterial cream for blisters, painkillers and allergy medications, teas for inducing sleepiness, and electrolyte powder for staying hydrated.

- Speaking of hydration, it can be difficult to stay hydrated and eat regularly when you're at a show. Pack snacks and a water bottle in your expo bag, and set a reminder on your phone to hydrate. Have snacks in your hotel room in case you didn't eat enough during the day and room service isn't an option.

After the event, a timely follow-up can cement the connections you made. Consider sending out thank-you emails, sharing additional information about your products or services, sending a sample, and scheduling a follow-up meeting with a clear agenda. This post–trade show engagement is just as crucial as your participation during the event in nurturing these nascent relationships.

EXHIBITING AT A TRADE SHOW

A QUICK CAVEAT

One of my favorite events is JEC World, the international composites trade show hosted annually in Paris. When I say this event is large, I mean it: it's more like a sprawling metropolis than a product showcase. At most trade shows, a map is a courtesy stuffed in your welcome bag. At JEC, it's a vital tool for navigation.

The organizations that exhibit at JEC hail from all corners of the globe. Most bring their A-game in the form of spectacular booths featuring innovative designs, vibrant lighting, and captivating product demos. These impressive displays—many of them more like an interactive science museum than a trade show booth—boast immersive experiences, cutting-edge multimedia displays, interactive demonstrations, and even cafés and bars. Each one is staffed by professionals armed with answers designed to impress and engage.

But there are always exceptions. The truth is, while many exhibits are great, others are ineffectively planned and executed, and it shows—both to the eye and in ROI. This applies to every trade show, not just JEC. So before we delve into the nuances of crafting an effective trade show presence, I'll issue a warning right up front: don't invest in a trade show unless you can do it well. Trade show exhibits are time and labor intensive. They require expertise and creativity, and they're expensive, even on a small scale. If you *can't* do it well, your marketing money and time would be better spent elsewhere. This is doubly true if you are the steward of someone else's money (such as that of taxpayers or investors).

Here are some examples, based on my own experience and industry best practices, of what makes a trade show exhibit universally ineffective:

- No description whatsoever of what your organization or product does. Attendees are not psychic.
- For companies that sell or design products, not providing examples of these products. More often than not, your customers will need to "see it to believe it."
- No lead capture system. What are you exhibiting for if not capturing leads?
- Wrinkled backdrops and tablecloths, pixelated graphics, or—even worse—stock images with visible watermarks that show the image was not paid for. Add to this: nonfunctioning videos and demos. All these things undermine your credibility. Do you want your current and prospective customers to think you are careless?
- Food, drinks, and a general "mess" throughout the booth (see above).
- An unstaffed booth. Alternatively, its close cousin: a booth with staff who appear tired or bored or who spend the entire show engrossed in their phones. Again, what are you at the show for if not interacting with your target audience?

- Obviously expensive booth hardware and furniture, but with any of the above. Cognitive dissonance is real. Also, if your organization is funded by other people, you are spending their money—not yours. Spend it wisely.

You might say, "We don't have the budget for a professional graphic designer or a booth architect. I don't know anything about event logistics for big shows. But we *must* be at this show!"

That's understandable. I want to emphasize that I'm not here to dissuade anyone from participating in a trade show; in fact, I whole-heartedly encourage it when it aligns with your goals. Trade shows offer incredible opportunities if approached strategically.

However, it's important to recognize that exhibiting at a trade show isn't without its challenges. It's an investment that requires many resources to do well. If done inadequately, your investment might not yield the desired results, affecting both your ROI and your brand's reputation. You want to engage with your target audience, capture leads, and leave a lasting impression. As you contemplate your participation, assess whether you have the necessary resources—whether that be time, personnel, or financial backing—to create an exhibit that truly represents your organization, resonates with your audience, and promotes your goals.

SO YOU'VE DECIDED TO MOVE AHEAD

This year, your organization has decided to have a booth at a trade show. Congratulations—this is a big deal! The importance of having a booth at a show cannot be overstated. This is your moment to shine, to demonstrate your products or research in a venue that buzzes with potential customers, partners, and competitors. Your booth is a physical embodiment of your brand, facilitating direct engagement and immediate feedback. It provides an unparalleled opportunity to demonstrate value, gather leads, and make lasting impressions on a receptive audience.

No pressure or anything.

Let's assume that this show was chosen logically and that your organization is committed to maximizing its return on this investment.

To begin, you'll start by creating a brief for this show. If the show objectives are clear, then your target audience and messaging should match. Examples of typical trade show objectives include acquiring a target number of sales and marketing leads, selling a specific quantity of product, or closing a specific deal. Other campaigns' objectives may intersect with this show's objectives, such as if you are attending this event as part of a broader product launch campaign. Avoid setting objectives that are difficult to quantify, or you may have difficulty justifying the potential impact of future events in your next budgeting round.

Other sections that you'll want to include in your show brief include any details that might be relevant to designers or the team eventually working in the booth, such as the following:

- Budget
- Booth design requirements, both functional and aesthetic
- How the booth space will be used throughout the show, such as for meetings, product demonstrations, or an in-booth café or bar

Since many of your decisions about your campaign and booth design will be driven by what you can afford, I'd like to focus on budget for a moment.

BUDGET

Remember how I mentioned that trade shows are expensive? Let's break that down. Here are your major considerations:

- Floor space
- Booth design
- Campaign considerations and assets
- Show services and other logistics
- Staff and travel

I. FLOOR SPACE

To register for an exhibit space, you must first select where you want to exhibit on the show floor. This decision drives your booth registration fee. You'll need to consider both the booth size, configuration, and location within the exhibit hall. In the US, trade show floor space is sold by the square foot (internationally, usually by the square meter) and, as of this printing, can run between USD$35 and USD$75 per square foot. Your location can also affect your rate. Most booths in the US are sold as either "in-line" (i.e., in a row of other booths side by side, along an aisle and usually sold in ten-foot-by-ten-foot incre-ments) or "island" (i.e., standalone spaces on the show floor and sold in larger sizes that usually start at twenty feet by twenty feet). In-line booths on the corners of aisles are typically more expensive.

Space in "start-up pavilions" is often less expensive than in the rest of the hall. If your budget is modest, contact your state's economic development or international trade departments, or your local univer-sity's sponsored research or industrial cooperation departments, to see if a group is sponsoring a "coalition" booth where you can buy a fraction of square footage in, for example, the "State of New Jersey" pavilion.

Your final site selection influences foot traffic and visibility. While there's no one-size-fits-all answer to the perfect booth location, certain factors can guide your decision. The prime spots are often near entrances, along main aisles, and near food and beverage stations—all places where foot traffic is high. However, these high-traffic areas can also be noisy and sometimes crowded. Furthermore, these prime spots usually come with a higher price tag and sell out quickly. You may also want to locate your competitors and customers on the floor plan and determine how close you want to be. Balance your budget with the anticipated benefits and trade-offs of each location.

II. BOOTH DESIGN

Once you've paid your booth registration fee, the show organizers will send you an exhibitor manual. This provides the necessary information and resources you'll need for show planning, including:

- Guidelines for booth design and setup, including when exhibitors are allowed to set up and tear down their booths
- Rules and regulations of the venue
- Shipping and material-handling instructions
- Details on how to order booth services, such as electricity, rigging, lead retrieval, and A/V packages
- Order forms and instructions for ordering additional services, such as catering for in-booth events
- Other logistical information

You'll need this information to start thinking about your booth design. Regardless of your booth size, you should likely hire a professional to design your booth. Much can go wrong in terms of the interior design of the floor plan and any graphics that must be made. As you work with a professional, there are some important considerations you should keep in mind as you select your designer and create a design together.

Let's start with what sort of display you need. If you have a small in-line space and a small budget, there are vendors online that provide professional yet simple setups. These displays offer several benefits:

- The displays tend to be inexpensive (as of this writing, between USD$500 and USD$2,500).
- You can often find displays with additional features, such as a shipping case that converts to a display counter, backlighting kits, and the ability to hold graphics printed on multiple materials.
- They can be set up by two people without hiring additional labor from the venue, which can be expensive.
- Many displays are designed to allow you to swap in and out booth graphics easily. This means that one set of display hardware could be used by multiple product teams or research units.
- Most offer easy-to-understand printer specifications and templates that you should give to your designer.

With a larger budget, you can work with specialized booth design companies that lease or sell you the hardware setup for an entire booth. You can find these companies online and browse their catalogs. Some trade show venues conveniently offer this service as well, and if it's available, it should be included in your exhibitor manual. These more elaborate displays offer several benefits:

- Since they were often designed by professional booth architects and then mass produced, they tend toward stylish, modern designs offered at a lower price than custom exhibits.

- These "all-in-one" kits contain most everything you need: the backdrop, flooring, collateral stands, counters and tables, display cases, stools and chairs, and other furniture appropriate to the layout.
- If purchasing is an option for you, many of these setups are designed to be modular, offering you a single display kit that can be used for multiple layouts and square footages.

Before meeting with your designer, read the exhibit manual so that you understand what you are allowed to do in your exhibit space. For example, many venues do not allow hanging signs in specific areas of the hall or for certain booth configurations. Be able to provide your designer with the applicable rules for your booth space and an exhibit hall map that clearly shows where your booth space will be located.

If you have other requirements, make sure to note them for your designer. These might be simple, such as requesting a dedicated flat surface of a specific size for a product demo, or they can be more complex, such as including several pieces of working equipment or a functional second story with a VIP meeting room. If you are bringing equipment, include the dimensions and electrical requirements for each in the brief. Tell your designer if you have anything else relevant happening at the show that could possibly affect your floor plan, such as a catered in-booth event or dedicated podcasting area.

Your designer will want to know how much creative leeway they have: Are they developing the concept from your napkin sketches, or do they have complete freedom within the confines of your show brief? If you have a concept in mind, be as illustrative as possible. Using artificial intelligence, such as DALL-E or Midjourney, can be an efficient way to generate rough concepts. Include specifics such as dimensions, your organization type, color scheme, audience, and other (nonconfidential) details in your prompt. If you'd rather your designer come up with concepts, that's fine too, but again, be clear with any specific elements you need in your booth. These could include a demonstration area, video screens, meeting spaces, room for an event, and other details of your brief. Have brand assets such as your logo and official colors ready.

Design decisions you make now can either save or cost you money. Remember that you won't only have to pay for the booth hardware and printing graphics; you'll also have to pay for shipping freight to and from the show, material handling, rigging, electrical, and so on. You can get an idea for what a typical exhibit might cost "all in" with some online research prior to your meeting. This way, you understand what your budget might bear for design elements and what it will not. ChatGPT or a Google search can give you an idea of cost based on your square footage and specific requirements. Rigged elements, such as hanging signs or projection equipment, are a significant cost driver. Likewise, any component that requires a lift, such as tall structures (e.g., towers, a second-story meeting space), or equipment that requires multiple electrical hookups, are other cost drivers to consider. If you can't afford it, make sure that your designer knows your budget constraints.

III. CAMPAIGN CONSIDERATIONS AND ASSETS

Put yourself in the shoes of the average trade show attendee: they've been walking all day. Their feet hurt. Their back aches. They either need more coffee or more water—they can't decide which, but they have a headache coming on and just consumed their last breath mint. There are six more booths to visit that day, and they want to hit the poster session before attending a team dinner that night.

There's a lot on the average attendee's mind as they approach your booth. How are you going to attract them?

When it comes to presenting complex ideas and products—and driving foot traffic to your booth—creativity is key. Live demonstrations can be fascinating to watch, making your booth a hot spot on the show floor. Interactive presentations, videos, samples, or virtual reality experiences offer visitors a hands-on experience. A café or craft beer bar can be a lifesaver to attendees and help you hit your booth traffic goals. A simple bowl of mints or chocolates can be just as welcome.

Your show toolkit should include collateral, such as copies of posters or papers, product spec sheets, brochures, and branded giveaways. Don't forget a stack of business cards for all attendees: you'll be making lots of new friends, and you want to ensure they have something tangible to remember you by. If you are designing these assets de novo, you may again want to hire a professional designer for assistance. Be sure to be realistic in terms of schedule for the development of any assets and to factor printing into your show budget.

IV. SHOW SERVICES AND OTHER LOGISTICS

Once you have a booth design, you can order show services and handle other logistics. Follow the exhibitor manual guidelines for specifics, but in general you may need to order the following services from your show's online exhibitor portal:

1. **Shipping and materials handling:** You'll need to ship your booth materials to a warehouse. Large shows typically have an advance warehouse that is available for shipment receiving until a certain deadline and a show site. The advance warehouse charges lower fees. For small seminars, you might be shipping to a hotel or be asked to bring your display with you.

2. **Rigging:** If your display includes elements that need to be rigged, make sure that your designer provides you with a rigging diagram that aligns to the show's requirements.

3. **Electrical:** Similar to your rigging order, you'll want your designer to furnish you with an electrical diagram that includes outlet placement and power requirements.

4. **Other labor:** You may need to hire show-site labor for other reasons, such as steaming a fabric banner from a lift.

5. **Catering:** If you plan to serve food or drink in your booth, you likely need to order these through the venue's approved catering service.

6. **Flooring:** Depending on your show, you may need to bring (or order) carpeting or other flooring. Pro tip: spring for the extra padding.

7. **Lead retrieval:** You want an easy way to document and disseminate the contact information for the leads you generate at the show. Most shows offer rentals of dedicated name badge–scanning hardware or app licenses compatible with iOS and Android devices. You simply scan a badge and the contact information is saved in a database. You usually get your leads as a CSV file after the show closes.

Let me share a story from my early career, during my time at the Advanced Structures and Composites Center. We were preparing for a trade show and had developed a remarkable digital backdrop we affectionately named "The Beast" (because it was massive, of course). This six-LCD-screen video wall (networked to Mac Minis) could play video across any combination of screens. We had written the software, produced the video and animations—it was quite a marvel. However, we had overlooked a critical logistical factor: The Beast's weight. Our caution had led us to overengineer the steel frame, adding considerable heft. The shipping cost to get The Beast to its destination was prohibitively expensive.

And that's how I ended up driving a packed university motor-pool van from Maine to Washington, DC. It was a caffeine-fueled road trip that taught me the importance of anticipating and planning show details well in advance.

V. BOOTH STAFF AND TRAVEL

Don't forget to plan for your booth staff. An effectively staffed booth is dynamic, friendly, and attentive. Ensure your team members understand their roles, schedules, and responsibilities. You should conduct training to equip them with the necessary knowledge to engage with your audience at the booth and prepare them for the variety of questions and interactions they'll encounter.

Trade shows offer a prime opportunity for lead generation. Have a system in place for capturing and tracking leads, so that each interaction can be followed up effectively after the show. This could include renting a lead retrieval option from exhibitor services.

You'll want to factor into your budget staff travel costs, such as flights and ground transportation, hotel rooms, and a per diem for meals. Be sure that they understand your organization's travel policy, including how to handle expense reports.

Remember, your booth is not just a display—it's a launching pad for new relationships. Plan effectively to maximize your return on investment.

PLANNING AND PRODUCING YOUR OWN EVENTS (YES, YOU CAN!)

Putting on your own event at a trade show (e.g., a VIP dinner or networking reception) might sound like a task better left to large corporations with unlimited resources. But it's not the realm of a privileged few. In fact, you, too, can host an event, and there can be significant benefits for science organizations in doing so. Your target audience is gathered for the show already—why not get them in a room of your own design?

Hosting your own event allows you to create a tailored experience focused solely on your niche, opening a channel to engage your audience and increase your visibility. Moreover, you get the chance to present your innovations, drive meaningful conversations, and position your organization as a thought leader to a captive audience.

Given the sheer range of events you could host, it would be impossible to outline a step-by-step process that accounts for each detail (indeed, event management is an elaborate specialty of its own). What follows, then, are some general insights and from-the-trenches advice to get you started.

1. **Plan further in advance than you think:** It's crucial to initiate the planning process well in advance. Once you have a target date in mind, you can start looking for a location. Depending on the scale of your event, you might consider booking a room at the trade show convention center, a nearby hotel, or a bar or restaurant. Along with venue selection, get the rest of your logistics in order: catering, décor, AV requirements, floor plan, traffic flow, and other details. Work with a professional event planner, if necessary.

2. **Consider selecting a theme:** It's more fun and memorable if there is a theme, and it gives you an anchor point for catering and design decisions.

3. **Know how you'll attract attendees:** Is it an invite-only event? Make sure to get RSVPs. Is it a "more the merrier"

occasion? Then build in time to plan and execute your promotional strategy.

4. **Manage risk:** Last but not least, plan contingencies. Potential issues could range from natural disasters to sudden entertainment cancellations, technical glitches, or changes in public health guidelines. Having a risk management plan in place will help you respond effectively to any unexpected events and ensure the safety and satisfaction of your attendees.

PODIUM PRESENTATIONS

At some point in your science marketing efforts, you may have to speak in front of a crowd. If you've been accepted to present at a conference, for example, this section is for you.

First, let's address a common fear: stage fright. Nearly everyone has it. When nerves become overwhelming, there are a few things you can do to regain control. Understand that it's completely natural to feel anxious when stepping up to the podium. Deep-breathing exercises can help calm the mind, while visualizing a successful presentation can instill a sense of confidence. Another beneficial approach is to shift your focus from yourself to the value you're providing to your audience. This outward focus can alleviate self-consciousness and help you deliver your message more effectively. Make sure to practice your presentation in front of a live audience. The difference between a presenter who has practiced and one who hasn't can be painfully obvious to the audience.

A common tool in the public speaker's arsenal is the PowerPoint presentation. However, it's important to use PowerPoint to enhance rather than detract from your message. While visuals are important, scientific presentations often require text. Keep slides clean and straightforward by sticking to the "six-six-six" rule—no more than six words per bullet point, six bullet points per slide, and six text-heavy slides in a row. Videos can be a great addition if they support your message, but they are notorious for glitching. Remember, your slides are a guide, not a script, so refrain from simply reading from them. Engage with your audience by speaking directly to them and use your slides as a backdrop to your narrative. Importantly, always be prepared for a computer crash—have backups of your presentation and be ready to continue without slides, if necessary.

As always, preparation is the key to a successful presentation. Practice your full presentation with your slides as many times as possible and make sure you're comfortable with the flow and content. This will not only increase your confidence but will also ensure you deliver a smooth and professional presentation.

Beyond these basic elements, there are a few additional insights I'd like to impart. These aren't hidden secrets, but I wish more science marketers took them to heart when preparing for a presentation. Storytelling, for instance, is a powerful tool in public speaking. People naturally relate to and remember stories, so use this to your advantage by weaving narratives into your talk. Analogies can also be highly effective in simplifying complex concepts, making them accessible and relatable to your audience. Visuals can illustrate results or complex ideas, but remember to keep them clear and straightforward.

THE SUCCESS OF A TRADE SHOW CAMPAIGN HINGES ON STRATEGIC PLANNING, METICULOUS EXECUTION, AND A COMMITMENT TO SEIZING OPPORTUNITIES.

Audience interaction is also important. Techniques such as direct questioning and polling can help keep your audience engaged and make your presentation more memorable. Finally, managing a question-and-answer session effectively can cement the positive impression you've worked hard to create. Prepare for questions and always answer with honesty and confidence. Remember, feedback, whether positive or negative, is a tool for growth.

The success of a trade show campaign hinges on strategic planning, meticulous execution, and a commitment to seizing opportunities. Whether demonstrating a groundbreaking innovation, forging new partnerships, or gaining insights into the pulse of the industry, the preparation and passion you bring to trade shows will shape the outcomes. The insights shared in this chapter offer a blueprint for harnessing the full potential of trade shows and turning them into a powerful asset in achieving your marketing goals.

With a clear understanding of your objectives and a well-crafted strategy, you can transform these bustling exhibition halls into fertile grounds for business development, collaboration, and innovation. From planning and designing your booth to engaging with attendees and making those essential after-hour connections, every aspect requires careful consideration and alignment with your brand's core values and vision. Leveraging these events effectively empowers you to drive your marketing strategy forward, cultivate meaningful relationships, and help establish or reinforce your position in the market.

KEY TAKEAWAYS

1. Trade shows are important and unique opportunities for networking, demonstrating complex products, and staying updated with industry trends. These events enable direct engagement with your target audience and provide a platform for marketers to highlight their products' distinctive features and for researchers to demonstrate the relevancy of their research.

2. To extract value from a trade show as an attendee, proactive planning and follow-up are crucial. Beyond appreciating the exhibits, align your interactions with the show objectives, such as generating sales leads or nurturing a partnership. Cultivate professional relationships through networking, learn to deliver a compelling elevator pitch, and prioritize follow-up communications.

3. Planning and hosting your own event is a significant yet attainable endeavor that can offer substantial benefits. This initiative enables you to tailor an event around your niche, significantly increasing your brand's visibility, fostering meaningful industry conversations, and providing a unique platform to present your scientific innovations.

4. Your trade show booth embodies your brand and facilitates direct engagement with your target audience, making booth space location selection, design, and budget all essential considerations. A well-crafted and thoughtfully positioned booth attracts foot traffic and visibility, facilitates conversations, enhances demonstrations, and helps generate valuable leads.

5. The human element of your booth (i.e., your staff) plays a vital role in your trade show success. Ensure they are well trained, understand their roles, and are prepared for a variety of interactions.

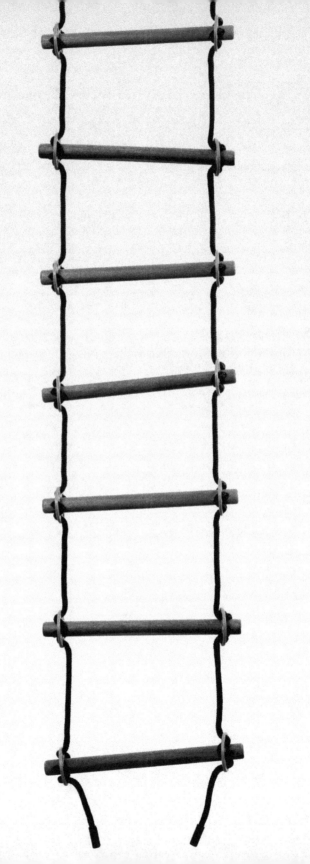

DATA-DRIVEN DECISIONS: HARNESSING ANALYTICS IN SCIENCE MARKETING

Fusion energy technology represents the cutting edge of sustainable power. Within this field, imagine a revolutionary product: a compact fusion reactor designed for localized energy production, capable of transforming the way communities source their power. Marketing this breakthrough technology requires precision, insight, and a deep understanding of both the scientific landscape and the market needs.

Consider a campaign to introduce this compact fusion reactor to global energy providers. A month into the marketing efforts, you find that your budget is running low. To secure additional funding, you must provide data and analytics that detail the effectiveness of your strategies, your trajectory toward your goals, and insights into the market's readiness for such a disruptive technology.

Your manager examines your data and approves the request, impressed with your progress. As you propose new initiatives to target specific industries or regions, more data is requested to justify these ambitions, leading to a thoughtful and data-driven modification to the goals.

This is not mere intuition; it's leveraging data and analytics to guide every decision, from budget allocation to strategic positioning.

IN MARKETING, UNDERSTANDING AND UTILIZING ANALYTICS IS NOT AN OPTIONAL SKILL—IT'S ESSENTIAL.

In marketing, understanding and utilizing analytics is not an optional skill—it's essential. This chapter will explore how to use data and analytics to ensure that your marketing strategy aligns with the complexities and demands of the scientific community, particularly in the context of groundbreaking innovations such as the compact fusion reactor.

THE POWER OF ANALYTICS IN DRIVING DECISIONS

Marketing analytics is an essential component of effective marketing strategies. When marketing complex products and services, such as the value of a compact fusion reactor, it's important to gather and analyze the right data to identify marketing challenges and drive informed, evidence-based decisions.

"But can't I just wing it?" I hear you say. "Let's make assumptions and get to the fun part." Go right ahead, but while I'm on the record, my advice is this: don't skip this. Analytics allows you to understand the effectiveness of your marketing efforts. It tells you what's working and what isn't, and it provides a clearer view of your audience's preferences and behaviors. All of this helps identify gaps in your strategies and empowers you to adjust.

Let's go back to our hypothetical marketing strategy for the compact fusion reactor designed for localized energy production.

Through analytics, the marketing team discovered that a significant portion of their target audience lived in regions struggling with energy sustainability. Armed with this insight, they were able to concentrate their marketing efforts on showcasing the reactor's potential to transform local energy sourcing. This data-driven approach maximized the impact of the campaign by also demonstrating the company's understanding of its potential customers' unique needs.

Armed with the right data, you have the power to craft personalized marketing campaigns, optimize customer journeys, allocate resources more efficiently, and ultimately improve the return on your organization's marketing investment. Otherwise, you'd be shooting in the dark (or playing darts blindfolded—pick your analogy).

Importantly, analytics isn't only a tool for reflection. It's also a guide for action. In science marketing, where the products and services can be complex and highly specialized, the role of analytics becomes even more important. By translating raw data into actionable insights, analytics is a powerful ally.

THE MARKETING FUNNEL

Let's talk about the marketing funnel. It's a critical model in the marketing world, and it's important in the context of analytics. Essentially, this model traces the customer's journey from their initial interaction with your brand, right through to conversion—the point at which they make a purchase or take some other significant action. There are many versions of the marketing funnel out there, all modified by marketers to fit their goals, but I want to focus on four key stages that are common to nearly all of them:

AWARENESS
This is where your potential customers first encounter your brand or product.

CONSIDERATION
Your potential customers have identified a need or problem
that your product might solve, and they're evaluating your solution among others.

CONVERSION
This is where your prospects decide to become customers and
complete a purchase or perform some other significant action.

REPEAT CONVERSION
They purchase from you again and again and, perhaps,
recommend your brand to others.

At each stage of the funnel, there are different metrics that you can examine to understand how effectively your leads transition from one stage to the next. By leveraging this information, you can identify if (and where) your leads are dropping out of the funnel and figure out what to do about it. For example, if a significant number of leads are aware of your research organization's membership program (i.e., they have signed up for and opened your membership drive campaign emails), but very few are considering it (i.e., they haven't engaged with specific content, such as the membership benefits page on your website or adding the membership to their shopping cart), this could indicate a disconnect in your messaging, a problem with the channels you're using to communicate, or your leads may not be the right ones.

Conversely, if leads are considering your membership program but aren't converting, it might be time to reevaluate your pricing strategy, your checkout process, or something else.

Analytics and the marketing funnel are intertwined. Analytics provides the data-driven insight to understand your marketing funnel's performance. It shows you where your strategy works and where it needs adjustment. This allows you to optimize your marketing efforts at each stage of the funnel, improving the lead's journey and, ultimately, your conversion rate.

KEY PERFORMANCE INDICATORS

But how do you *know*? After all, it's not like the funnel is a real thing that you can observe. Wouldn't it be helpful to have, well…some sort of indicator?

Fortunately, much like in other disciplines, marketing has tried-and-true key performance indicators (KPIs) that we use to evaluate the success of a campaign or tactic. Before we can determine how to use that information, I'll introduce a few key terms. Each item on this list represents a KPI—a metric that can gauge the effectiveness of certain marketing efforts. Not all of them will be relevant to your marketing strategy or organization, but they are generally some of the most useful and common. Even if I don't directly reference all of these in this chapter, rest assured that they'll surface as you delve deeper into marketing analytics.

- **# of marketing qualified leads (MQL):** A lead who has shown enough engagement with a company's marketing efforts to suggest a higher likelihood of becoming a customer when compared to other leads. MQLs have typically interacted with the company's content (e.g., opened an email, downloaded a white paper, attended a webinar) and are considered ready for the next stage in the sales process. The next stage could be a specific nurture program on the topic they've shown interest in or simply adding points to their lead score as they interact with more marketing material until they score high enough—by showing enough interest—to become a sales qualified lead.

- **# of sales qualified leads (SQL):** A prospective customer who has been researched and vetted by both the marketing team and the sales team and is deemed ready for the next stage in the sales process. Sometimes a lead is deemed "sales qualified" based on an automated lead scoring system, such as the one described above. Certain interactions can cause a lead to be considered an SQL automatically, such as requesting a demonstration or sample. The distinction between an MQL and an SQL lies in the readiness to buy: an SQL is considered further along in the purchasing journey than an MQL, and it is time for them to interact with the sales team.

- **Marketing attribution:** The process of identifying which marketing activities contribute to sales and revenue. It helps marketers understand which channels, campaigns, or tactics are most effective in driving conversions, customer acquisition, revenue, and repeat engagement.

- **New lead rate (traffic-to-lead ratio):** This metric measures the effectiveness of a website in converting visitors into leads. It is calculated by dividing the number of new leads by the total number of visitors (traffic) over a certain period.

- **Landing page conversion rate:** This is the percentage of people who complete a desired action (like filling out a form or making a purchase) on a landing page out of the total number of people who visited the page.

- **Traffic sources and corresponding conversion rates:** Traffic sources refer to where website visitors are coming from, such as organic search, social media, email campaigns, or paid advertising. The corresponding conversion rate is the percentage of visitors from each source that complete a desired action.

- **Customer acquisition cost:** The total cost of attracting a customer to purchase a product or service. It includes costs associated with marketing and sales efforts, and it is calculated by dividing total acquisition costs by the number of new customers during a specific period.

- **Customer lifetime value:** This is the projected revenue a company expects to generate from a customer over the duration of their relationship with the business. It helps companies understand how much they can spend on acquiring new customers and retaining existing ones.

- **Open rate:** In email marketing, the "open rate" is the percentage of recipients who open a particular email out of the total number of emails sent.

- **Click-through rate (CTR):** The ratio of users who click on a specific link to the number of total users who view a page, email, or advertisement. It's often used to measure the success of an online advertising campaign.

- **Website traffic metrics:** These are statistics that show how users interact with a website, such as the number of sessions, pages per session, which traffic sources drive sessions, session duration, and conversion rate.

YOUR ANALYTICS-ENABLING TECHNOLOGY STACK

Now let's talk about how to get this information into a format that you can draw insights from. A "technology stack" is a group of software tools that work together to achieve a goal. A marketing analytics-enabling technology stack comprises various tools and platforms used to collect, process, and analyze relevant marketing data. The resulting information can be presented on interactive dashboards in easily digestible charts and lists to provide insights that can aid in strategic decision-making.

The analytics space is ever evolving, and the tools and practices that are relevant today might not be tomorrow. Considering these dynamics, it's possible that by the time you are reading this, some of the tools I reference in this chapter may no longer exist or be relevant. New ones may have emerged. Best practices, too, may have changed. When developing your own analytics strategy, I encourage you to use this chapter as a starting point for developing a process and do your own research into the tools available to you.

Here are the components that constitute a basic analytics-enabling technology stack:

I. ACCESS TO KEY PLATFORMS

To begin with, you'll need access to the platforms that you, or your organization, use to manage your marketing channels. Typical platforms include the website's content management system (CMS), social channels, the customer relationship management system (CRM), advertising platforms, and marketing automation platform for email marketing, social post scheduling, lead capture forms, and other campaign tools.

Access to these platforms ensures that you can connect various analytics tools to them to track and analyze the effectiveness of your interactions.

II. WEBSITE ANALYTICS

Arguably, the most significant component of an analytics-enabling tech stack is the website analytics tool. More often than not, your website is your primary "owned" channel. Many of your campaigns may start and even end on your website. But what are visitors actually doing there? Are they just landing on the home page and then leaving before any meaningful engagement takes place? Are they visiting a conversion-oriented landing page and leaving before converting?

Google Analytics and similar services offer free user analytics tools that track and capture website data to analyze user interactions on your site. You probably already have Google Analytics or a similar product set up (most site developers today install and configure it as a standard part of website development projects). If not, you should contact your web developer and have that done.

On a basic level, Google Analytics helps you determine:

- Traffic to important pages
- Engagement metrics
- Most frequented pages
- How the site was discovered
- Visitor paths
- Geographical origin of visitors
- The devices, operating systems, and browsers used
- Conversion actions
- And more

This wealth of information can already provide valuable insights, especially when narrowed to a specific time frame and compared to another. Note that if your Google Advertising account is not linked to your Google Analytics account, your ad spend won't show up properly in Google Analytics. If you are new to Google's analytics tools, Google offers free training that you should take to become familiar.

Google offers two more tools that you might not have set up yet:

- **Google Search Console** ensures that your site is properly crawled and indexed by Google. It also helps identify and address issues that impact the technical performance and search equity of your site.
- **Google Tag Manager**, on the other hand, reports on conversions and other event data, and manages integrations with other software.

It's important that these accounts are set up and are pulling data. Utilizing these tools in tandem, you can build a comprehensive understanding of your website's performance, allowing you to enhance your marketing strategies and ultimately improve your results.

III. SEO TRACKING TOOLS

Search engine optimization is the process of optimizing your webpage so that it appears prominently in relevant search results. It's a critical component of most effective marketing strategies. To optimize your site and improve its search engine rankings, you need to utilize SEO tracking tools. Today's subscription-based tools—popular options include Semrush, Ahrefs, and Moz Pro—provide invaluable insights into how well your website is optimized for search, allowing you to understand what's working well and identify areas that need improvement.

One of the primary functions of SEO tracking tools is to provide information on keyword performance. The keywords you care about are the words and phrases your target audience types into search engines when they want to find products (or research, or services, or organizations) like yours. You want to know what those words are, and you want to know how well the corresponding pages on your website rank for them—where in search results does your website appear? These tools allow you to identify new keywords so that you know what keywords are important. They can also analyze your website and tell you how to improve your ranking for a particular keyword you're tracking, as well as tell you which websites currently rank well (this is your competition).

Another thing to consider—and an aspect that SEO tracking tools help you manage and optimize—are backlinks. Backlinks are links from external websites that point to your site, and they play a significant role in search engine rankings. These tools allow you to analyze your backlink profile by providing information on the quantity and quality of your backlinks. You can identify which websites are linking to yours, evaluate their authority and relevance, and monitor the growth and impact of your backlink profile over time. This insight helps you refine your backlink building strategies and strengthen your website's authority in the eyes of search engines. Your authority rating plays a role in how well your website ranks in search across the board.

Your website's authority rating is also influenced by its technical performance on a battery of tests of its speed, XML sitemaps, robots.txt file, structured data, and mobile responsiveness. Yet resolving technical issues with your website doesn't only improve your search ranking. It's also important for user experience. For instance, site speed not only impacts how search engines rank a site but also how users perceive its usability and reliability. Similarly, mobile optimization is crucial, as a growing number of users access content via mobile devices. A website that isn't mobile friendly can frustrate users, leading to lower engagement. Structured data, while directly aiding search engines in understanding content context, also plays a role in enhancing rich snippets in search results, thereby improving click-through rates. In essence, optimizing for technical SEO often goes hand in hand with enhancing the overall user experience. Platforms such as Semrush and Ahrefs are invaluable for tracking technical SEO elements because they offer insights into site health, identify crawl issues, and provide recommendations for optimization.

Yet another feature offered by SEO tracking tools is competitive analysis. These tools enable you to evaluate your competitors' websites, analyze their SEO strategies, and identify opportunities to gain a competitive edge. You can compare keyword rankings, backlink profiles, content strategies, and other key metrics to benchmark your performance against your competitors. By understanding what your competitors are doing well and identifying areas where they are falling short, you can refine your own SEO approach and capitalize on untapped opportunities.

Importantly, these tools help you produce reports that tell you how well your website performs in organic search overall, versus your competitors, and for specific keywords over time, which is how you'll know whether your SEO strategy is working or not.

IV. INTERPRETATION AND REPORTING

Given the wealth of data generated by these tools, a reporting solution such as Databox can help bring everything together for comprehensive interpretation. This tool allows you to create customized dashboards that aggregate data from different sources, helping you visualize and understand data more effectively, and thereby drive better-informed decision-making. For example, you could create a dashboard that monitors the KPIs for a specific campaign.

HOW IT ALL CONNECTS: FUSION REACTOR CAMPAIGN ANALYTICS

When marketing a product as groundbreaking and complex as a compact fusion reactor, the right analytics-enabling technology stack plays a vital role in understanding the audience and crafting targeted strategies. Here are ways the fusion reaction company's marketing team used its analytics technology stack:

- By using Google Analytics, the team was able to identify which geographical regions showed the most interest in sustainable energy solutions. This insight guided their PPC advertising strategies to help them target those specific areas.
- The team's SEO tracking tool provided data on popular keywords related to fusion energy. This helped in optimizing content that not only ranked higher in search engines but also resonated with the scientific community, regulators, and energy enthusiasts.
- The competitive analysis feature offered by their SEO tracking tool enabled the marketing team to gauge the strategies of competitors in the fusion technology space, allowing them to find unique angles and untapped opportunities.
- Using an integrated KPI dashboard, the team was able to visualize all these insights, aligning them with campaign goals.

This example illustrates how the technology stack isn't just a collection of tools but an interconnected system that provides actionable insights tailored to specific marketing challenges.

VARIABLES THAT MATTER FOR DRIVING RESULTS

Part of being a science marketer (and now, a data-driven science marketer!) is the constant search for solutions to problems—problems that impede our ability to reach and persuade our target audience effectively. Analytics is part of our toolkit for solving those problems because it measures the reaction to marketing variables.

> PART OF BEING A SCIENCE MARKETER (AND NOW, A DATA-DRIVEN SCIENCE MARKETER!) IS THE CONSTANT SEARCH FOR SOLUTIONS TO PROBLEMS.

The manipulation of marketing variables influences specific outcomes. These variables are specific aspects of a campaign or asset that can be manipulated to optimize outcomes in different marketing areas, such as website search equity, email campaign performance, and social channel engagement. Example variables include audience targeting in paid advertising campaigns, subject lines in emails, and call-to-action buttons on landing pages. The tools I discussed earlier provide the data to help you decide which variables to adjust, when to adjust them, and how hard. The table below captures how these concepts are intertwined.

MARKETING CHALLENGE	EXAMPLE VARIABLES TO EXPLORE	OUTCOMES INFLUENCED	RECOMMENDED TOOLS/ STRATEGIES
Low organic search traffic to website	Keyword strategy, content quality, website speed	SERP ranking, organic traffic	SEO tracking platform, Google Analytics, Google Tag Manager, Google Search Console, content strategy
Low email open rate	Subject line, email database quality	Open rate, click-through rate	Subject line A/B testing, remove unengaged contacts, review deliverability data
Low engagement on social channels	Content quality, post cadence, audience targeting	Engagement, relevant follower growth, website traffic	Analytics dashboard, scheduled posting, engagement strategy, content strategy

A marketer adjusts these variables to resolve challenges and maximize results. By understanding what each lever does and how it influences your marketing outcomes, you can create a custom solution for virtually any problem you encounter. You use the clues your data provides to form a hypothesis, test it, and then analyze the results.

However amazing that sounds, here's a counterbalance: many of the market segments you operate in are small. This means that our sample size for any given data set might be too small to comfortably draw conclusions or might take too long to grow large enough for the conclusions to matter. This means that—quite unlike marketing to large audiences, as you would if you worked at Nike or Netflix— we often don't have enough data fast enough to make testing call-to-action tags or hero image options realistically worth it. Having someone on your team who has experience with what (generally) works and what (generally) doesn't is invaluable in these situations.

In this section, we will explore some common problems that science marketers face and discuss which variables you might consider manipulating to address them. The goal, however, is not to provide a one-size-fits-all solution or detailed guide to analytics interpretation. This chapter is meant to equip you with a toolkit to think critically and creatively about your marketing challenges and how you might solve them.

I. SEARCH EQUITY

An entire book could be devoted to the intricate, ever-changing subject of enhancing your search equity. This is not that book. However, I'll condense the essentials here. Despite its nuanced nature and fluidity, the primary challenge has consistently been the same for over a decade: How do you ensure that your product rises to the top of the search results when potential customers input specific keywords as searches?

A "search engine results page" (SERP) is a fancy term for the page you see after entering a word or phrase into a search engine. Your SERP equity hinges on a myriad of elements, including the relevance and quality of your content. Google and other search engines prize meaningful, high-quality content that effectively addresses your target audience's needs. Therefore, investing in the creation of that content will naturally boost your organic search ranking over time.

Tactically speaking, I have two recommendations to do this effectively:

1. **Start now:** You should write your website's text (called "copy") with relevant keywords for each page in mind. Don't just create a page for your primary service without identifying what your ideal customer would search for to find that page.

2. **Improve over time:** At least once a year, develop a calendar of new web pages, blogs, articles, case studies, and other text-based content you want to create that year. Base this at least in part on what relevant keywords your customers are using but you aren't ranking for.

Assuming your website domain hasn't been blacklisted and the site itself is devoid of significant technical hitches, SEO campaigns often begin by collating a list of terms that resonate with the particular campaign audience in question. Following this, the baseline "gap" between your equity for these terms and its SERP competitors is established. This is used as a guide to hone existing web-based resources such as landing pages to align with these pivotal terms or to develop new content written with those keywords in mind from the beginning.

Tools such as Moz Pro and Ahrefs assist in identifying SERP competitors, gauging keyword competitiveness, and providing a thorough analysis of your site's search traffic. However, patience is key. The journey to the top of search results can be painfully slow, especially when navigating competitive markets or contending with SERP competitors that have high domain authority.

Inevitably, there will be instances where search equity is lacking. Here, relying solely on organic reach might not deliver the desired results. It might be necessary to harness paid channels. Paid search ads—those "sponsored" snippets at the top of search result pages—can elevate your website traffic while you build its search equity over time. Consequently, your brand maintains a presence on relevant SERPs on search engines such as Google or Bing, even if it isn't the organic search placement you ultimately aspire to achieve. Alternatively, you can devise a groundbreaking guerrilla marketing campaign that will rattle the entire industry (good luck pitching *that* to your stakeholders!).

II. EMAIL CAMPAIGNS

This next section is of most use for those of you who use a marketing automation platform or website plug-in to send marketing emails. For example, you might use Mailchimp to send a monthly newsletter, or send monthly promotional emails to your mailing list from the back end of your e-commerce system.

We measure a marketing email's success with a handful of metrics. Your role is to interpret these results for strategic improvements.

- **Deliverability:** This tells you how effectively your campaign reaches recipients' inboxes. It is influenced by technical factors such as your DMARC (domain-based message authentication, reporting, and performance) and SPF (unauthorized email server) records, your sending domain's reputation, and the success of your emails in evading spam filters. Monitoring its deliverability requires vigilance. Regular domain checks on platforms such as MxToolbox can preempt significant issues. If deliverability becomes a concern, most marketing automation platforms offer free training on ways to address or chat with your organization's IT department.

- **Open rate:** The open rate represents the number of people who opened your email, which is influenced by your email's send time and the effectiveness of your subject line, among other factors. A compelling subject line can make the difference between an email being opened and ignored. Many marketing automation platforms offer native A/B testing. This works by sending a portion of your email list each of two email versions. Based on which performs better, the platform will automatically default to the winning and send it to the rest of the audience.

- **Click-through rate:** CTR tells you the percentage of email recipients who clicked on a link in your email. Achieving a high CTR demands compelling, personalized content that is relevant and appealing to the reader. Experimenting with personalization, such as using a recipient's first name or tailoring content to their specific needs and interests, can boost engagement.

- **Unsubscribes:** An unusually high or low unsubscribe rate could signal a larger issue, such as misaligned messaging or an audience that didn't opt into email sends. A healthy unsubscribe rate, however, can actually contribute to a more engaged database. You'd rather have people opt out of receiving your emails and thereby tell you that they aren't interested—information you can learn from—than leave them in the mix of interested people who aren't opening your emails and throwing off your data.

If your campaigns aren't delivering the metrics you anticipated, consider these steps:

- **Audience engagement:** Assess your audience's level of interest and engagement. If you're starting with a disinterested audience, your emails might be perceived as spam rather than valuable content. Clean your email list regularly by removing unengaged leads.

- **Message/audience alignment:** Ensure your campaign messages align with your audience's needs and interests. Narrowing your audience and customizing your messaging for each typically yields better results than generic messaging sent to broad audiences.

- **Design and UX:** Adhere to email design and UX best practices, such as ensuring compatibility with both mobile and desktop devices, and verify that special characters are displayed correctly. Unless you are doing something intentionally weird, stick to email layouts that "look like" what your readers are used to receiving from other organizations.

- **Clear call to action:** Include a clear, compelling CTA in your emails to drive your readers to act. Often this is a colorful button near where your reader puts their thumb while scrolling for easy access. A well-crafted CTA can significantly improve your click-through rate.

- **Testing:** Beyond subject lines, consider A/B testing other email components, such as CTAs, body copy, design elements, and send times to maximize engagement. Most email automation platforms offer free trainings on this topic.

If you are just starting out, you might not yet have a database of potential email recipients. You can develop your email list in many ways, and there are great resources online that delve into these strategies and tactics more deeply. Don't just go adding names to the database. Familiarize yourself with the CAN-SPAM Act, GDPR, and other relevant legislation that largely prohibits these practices.

Here are a few ways to deal with not having an email database:

1. **Rent a list for your campaign:** Email campaigns sent to lists rented from trade press or industry organizations can generate awareness, leads, and sales. The individuals on the lists may not be familiar with your organization, so their engagement with your email will hinge on how relevant they consider your email address and subject line when they see it in their inbox (to open it), and whether your email's content is timely and engaging enough to warrant a click. You can improve opens and clicks by only sending an email if you believe the message is relevant and engaging for this specific recipient list. Test your messaging thoroughly.

2. **Sponsor an event:** Many event sponsorships offer a similar service as a list rental. My recommendations above apply.

3. **Make subscribing to your list easy and do other marketing:** You don't have to send emails to a list from day one. Make it easy to subscribe to your list (e.g., put the subscription form in your website header). Then do other marketing while asking people to subscribe to your newsletter. For example, be a guest on a podcast, exhibit at a trade show, or write a bylined article for a relevant publication and use these as

opportunities to ask people to subscribe to your list. If you do this consistently, over time your list will grow.

III. SOCIAL CHANNELS

Like most other marketing channels, your social media performance can be tracked and evaluated. Like search engine metrics, social media can be split into two categories: "organic," which refers to engagement with your brand that you don't pay for, such as sharing a post on your company's LinkedIn page, and "paid," which are boosted posts or other paid ads to extend your reach beyond your follower count. Your follower count over time is one measure for determining the effectiveness of your social campaigns. Other metrics such as the quantity of likes, comments, and shares tell you how engaging your content is and whether you are posting when your audience is most likely to see it.

This data-driven view of your social activity can come at a cost of the true value of your social channels: engagement with your audience. If you are active on the same social channels as your target customer, for instance, you have a direct link to ask them questions and build relationships with them.

TRACKING THE LESS TRACKABLE: PODCASTS, PR, AND EVENTS

Tracking clicks on digital ads and in emails is relatively straightforward. But how do you track a key win, like when a key figure in your organization is quoted in a major nontrade publication such as the *New York Times*? Or when you make a guest appearance on an industry podcast? Those placements take work—often done by a publicist or PR agency—but don't necessarily translate directly to sales or website clicks.

I want to be clear: not every marketing endeavor will provide immediate, measurable ROI. In a landscape that relies heavily on the quantifiable, it's easy to overlook the value of activities that may raise the awareness and equity of your brand over time. However, you have more opportunities to track than you may think.

One way to gauge the impact of your campaigns—especially if you don't have a single automation platform to help you with this—is by using UTM codes, which are invaluable. This is doubly true if you need to measure traffic from an unowned channel, such as a partner organization's website or an ad in an online industry directory. UTM codes are add-ons to URLs, and they help you track your traffic from specific sources and easily pull that data into campaign-specific CSV files and data boards. Here's an example of what a URL with a UTM code looks like:

https://www.hightouchgroup.com/example?utm_campaign=post&utm_medium=social&utm_source=linkedin.

This URL showcases UTM codes in action. It breaks down your campaign name (utm_campaign=post), the channel (utm_medium=social), and the specific platform (utm_source=linkedin). When a user clicks on this UTM-encoded URL, each of these parameters is sent to your analytics dashboard, allowing you to track the source, medium, and campaign associated with the visitor's entry to your site. You can then shorten this URL using a branded URL shortener.

For print ads, where lengthy URLs are impractical and shortened URLs are difficult to remember, QR codes offer a potential solution. These scannable images bypass the need for URL memorization and are easily created using online generators.

Managing UTM and QR codes can be as simple as maintaining a shared spreadsheet with campaign URLs and QR images, or as using dedicated platforms that create and organize these per campaign.

Science marketing strategists should develop the ability to blend data with instinct. Experience, research, and intuition should guide the creative process, but the effectiveness of the campaign should be evaluated using data when possible. If a particular strategy or tactic isn't delivering as expected, don't make baseless assumptions: determine the root cause and adjust your strategy with full transparency and speed. This data-driven yet intuitive approach is key to maximizing the success of your marketing campaigns, but it isn't everything. Remember that doing your job well doesn't mean that every campaign is a slam dunk; it means that you watch and adjust as needed to make your overall marketing strategy a success.

A HYPOTHETICAL BIOTECHNOLOGY COMPANY'S MARKETING ANALYTICS TECHNOLOGY STACK

Let's imagine a biotechnology company, BioInnovate, Inc., which is launching a new line of lab equipment targeted at various research institutions. To optimize their marketing efforts, they want to understand how potential customers are interacting with their online promotional materials, product pages, social media ads, and email campaigns.

To accomplish this, BioInnovate's marketing team works with a digital agency to build an analytics-enabling technology stack comprising several interconnected tools:

1. **Customer relationship management software:** They use a CRM to track customer interactions and segment their audience into different categories based on the type of insti-

tutions (e.g., universities, private labs, government research centers).

2. **Web analytics tool:** Google Analytics is implemented to monitor website traffic, user behavior, and the effectiveness of different landing pages and content related to their lab equipment.

3. **Social media analytics platform:** A specialized tool like Sprout Social provides insights into their social media campaign performance, including audience engagement, demographics, and trends in sharing and commenting.

4. **Email marketing analytics:** A platform like Mailchimp allows them to track the success of email campaigns, including open rates, click-through rates, and conversion from email to product inquiries or sales.

5. **Data integration and visualization tool:** Finally, they utilize a platform like Tableau to integrate data from all these sources into interactive dashboards. These dashboards provide real-time insights, displaying easily digestible charts and lists that showcase KPIs, trends, and patterns.

By deploying this cohesive technology stack, BioInnovate is able to gain a comprehensive understanding of their marketing performance across various channels. They can identify the most effective content, determine where potential customers drop off in the sales funnel, and uncover insights that inform adjustments to their marketing strategies.

For example, through the dashboard, they notice that academic researchers are particularly interested in a specific feature of their equipment and are primarily engaging through LinkedIn posts. They then shift resources to create more targeted content for this audience on LinkedIn, leading to increased inquiries and sales within that segment.

This technology stack not only provides a holistic view of their marketing activities but also allows BioInnovate to make data-driven decisions, optimizing their marketing efforts for the science and research community and ensuring a successful launch for their new line of lab equipment.

KEY TAKEAWAYS

1. Analytics plays a crucial role in identifying what's working and what's not with your campaigns.

2. The marketing funnel and key performance indicators help you understand the effectiveness of your activities. The marketing funnel provides a framework to understand a lead's journey through your pipeline and identify areas for improvement. KPIs, on the other hand, are metrics that help evaluate the success of specific marketing activities. Understanding and tracking KPIs enable you to measure your campaign performance and optimize your overarching marketing strategy.

3. Manipulating variables refers to making strategic adjustments to the relevant variables of a campaign asset or tactic to achieve a specific result. By understanding the variables available and what they influence, marketers can make informed decisions to improve campaign results.

4. Earned media, brand mentions, and other "wins" for your organization contribute to brand visibility and reputation, even if their impact cannot be quantified directly in real time, unlike a marketing email.

A GLANCE BACKWARD, A STEP FORWARD

It's no secret that the world is changing rapidly. In many cases, technology and science are at the forefront of this evolution. Therefore, effective marketing for science products and innovations becomes not just a business necessity but a vehicle for societal transformation as well. Hopefully, now that you've reached the end of this journey, you can see just how potent a change agent effective marketing can be.

As we enter the final pages of this foray, I'd like to pause to reflect on what we've uncovered and learned. It's a good time to look back before we take our next steps forward.

In the beginning, we set the stage for success by diving deep into the complexities of our target audience. We sought to understand their concerns, motivations, and preferences. This allowed us to craft resonant messages, frame our core message, and carefully assess our marketing channels. The creation of a "value vow" emerged as a unique promise, a dynamic pledge to our audience that would guide our entire journey.

From there, we moved on to the art of storytelling. After all, our competitive landscape is filled with direct and indirect competitors, all vying for attention. We need to stand out. By infusing our brand's story with a consistent value vow and an engaging user experience, we shaped a narrative that wasn't just informative but deeply engaging.

Then came strategy—our blueprint for success. This chapter wasn't just about setting goals and understanding the market. It was about positioning our product, developing a unique value vow, and selecting the right channels. The creation of a backgrounder and marketing brief was more than documentation; it was about building a comprehensive vision. Especially in highly regulated markets, industry-specific insights honed our approach, making our strategies not just effective but uniquely tailored.

Next, creativity beckoned. Big ideas, resonant themes, and a blend of science with artistry allowed us to create campaigns that were not just visible but memorable. Channels became our conduits, the paths through which we reached our audience. Whether through innovative communication or strategic selection, we learned to adapt our message to various mediums. Our website, for example, became a powerful ambassador, a digital emissary conveying our value vow to the world.

Trade shows and public speaking opened up a world of personal connection and direct engagement. From planning our booth to networking and follow-up, we discovered that the human element was the key to success. Careful planning of our involvement provided visibility and a unique platform to showcase our innovations. Through careful booth design, strategic positioning, and engaged staff, we were able to turn these events into golden opportunities to generate leads and build relationships.

Finally, we laid the basis for our analytics strategy. We manipulated variables, monitored KPIs, and analyzed the marketing funnel to optimize our results. Even the less quantifiable wins, such as earned media, contributed to our brand's visibility and reputation. Analytics is not simply a tool; it's your compass that can guide you toward continuous improvement and excellence.

There are still a few things I'd like to impart, and I hope you'll indulge me before we say our goodbyes (and, speaking from a purely subjective point of view, I think you'll get something from it too).

ERRATA (A.K.A. STUFF WE DIDN'T COVER)

Marketing is a complex field. It's continually evolving and multifaceted. That said, there are some areas that warrant attention but didn't find their way into the main chapters of this book. These aspects provide additional insights that can further refine your marketing approach. Let's jump into a few of them.

"ALWAYS ON" MARKETING

In previous chapters, we talked a lot about campaigns: the importance of planning them, defining them, running them, evaluating them, and so on. But in the real world, campaigns don't live in a vacuum; there are often multiple campaigns happening at once. Then there are marketing activities that don't ever stop. This is called "always on" marketing. This type of marketing is always working in the background, maintaining a constant presence and nurturing relationships. It requires planning, execution, and continuous refinement.

Consider your website's SEO strategy. It's an important part of "always on" marketing. Yes, your campaigns need landing pages that are optimized for that campaign's goals. But your static website also needs an SEO strategy that works continually in the background to meet overarching, long-term goals. This means constant monitoring, adjustments, and a specific process for adapting to trends and changes in behavior.

Your website content creation takes on new dimensions viewed from this lens. It involves careful planning around specific trends and interests as well as creating content that's "evergreen" (i.e., content that won't be outdated in a year's time and can therefore exist on your website and attract visitors without having to think about it too much).

PUTTING OUT FIRES

Not all aspects of marketing are as calm and well planned as one might hope. It's important to know that you may at some point be required to put your "firefighter hat" on. In marketing (indeed, in many disciplines), a "fire" is an unexpected, potentially disastrous, and wholly unplanned-for flare-up of—something. It doesn't matter. It's a crisis. Who will be responsible for resolving this crisis? As the one overseeing the project, that responsibility likely falls to you.

Planning for a crisis is vital. This involves identifying potential weak points and creating an emergency plan with clear protocols, contact information, and backup systems. Regular monitoring, collaboration between departments, and training are key in maximizing avoidance through preparation.

When a crisis does occur (and believe me, despite your best-laid plans, one will), grace under pressure is essential. Immediate action, clear communication, and a calm response are required. In my experience, there are a few things that will make the whole process go smoother when the unwanted does happen:

- **Identify the crisis:** Determine the nature of the crisis and how it directly impacts the marketing strategy, brand reputation, or other essential elements.

- **Assemble a crisis team:** Pull together a team of key personnel, including public relations, marketing, legal, and scientific experts, to coordinate the response.

- **Assess the impact:** Gauge the potential impact on the brand, stakeholders, and scientific community. This may include reputational damage, financial loss, or misinformation.

- **Develop a clear message:** Create a concise, truthful, and science-based message that addresses the crisis and demonstrates responsibility and transparency.

- **Communicate with stakeholders:** Engage with all involved parties, including customers, partners, regulators, and the media. Provide consistent updates and information.

- **Implement immediate actions:** Depending on the nature of the crisis, start immediate, corrective measures such as recalling products, halting advertising, or updating incorrect information.

- **Monitor the situation:** Keep a close eye on how the situation evolves and how the public and stakeholders are reacting. Adjust the strategy as needed.

- **Evaluate and learn:** After the crisis has been resolved, you should conduct a thorough analysis to understand the root cause of what went wrong and how to prevent similar incidents in the future. Rather than dwelling on the experience, learn from it and implement any necessary changes.

Remember, the key is a prompt and well-coordinated response, grounded in accurate information and transparent communication.

RELATIONSHIPS

Marketing doesn't exist in isolation; it thrives on connections, both external and internal. I've touched on this in other parts of the book, but since so much of marketing is externally faced, I'd like to turn your eye back inward a bit.

Whether you're part of an in-house marketing team, an external consultant, a solo communications specialist, or the CEO of a start-up company, it's critical to build cross-departmental or cross-functional relationships. Managing relationships isn't just about grasping the complexities of products and making your own decisions. It's also about connecting different roles to advance the organization. It makes it easier for decision makers to see the impact of marketing. This approach encourages cohesive progress and a shared vision across various departments. It turns the complexity of science into an advantage, strengthening the organization's overall direction and success.

I'd like to share a few tips that can help marketers forge and maintain these relationships.

I. R&D AND PRODUCT OWNERS

Understandably, this team can often be protective of their work. They have intimate knowledge of the inner workings and have poured their best efforts into these projects. Meanwhile, it's your job as a marketer to promote and sell their creations. This task can sometimes lead to conflict, as the method you've determined to be most effective for marketing might not align with how they perceive their work should be represented. It can be disheartening for them to see their intricate work reduced to a few bullet points or simplistic messages. Therefore, building trust and collaboration is key to bridging these different perspectives.

Knowledge-sharing sessions can serve as a tremendous unifying force. Imagine the new marketing coordinator arranging for different departments to educate each other about their work. It not only gives them a quick immersion into the organization's workings but also helps other departments view the company's work through a different lens. This can help break down silos, foster mutual respect, and promote a holistic understanding of the company's work.

Building on this idea of knowledge-sharing, effective communication should be a two-way street. Regularly engaging in open dialogues and feedback sessions with R&D and product owners can promote a sense of partnership. Provide them with a voice in how their work is portrayed, ensuring that marketing strategies align with their values and insights. By embracing this collaboration, marketing can create more accurate and resonant messages, enhancing the authenticity of the brand. Ultimately, these relationships can lead to more effective marketing campaigns that honor the complexity and innovation of the work, driving success for the entire organization.

II. YOUR BOSS AND OTHER DECISION MAKERS

Marketing is synonymous with a near-constant selling of your strategies, creative ideas, and budgets to decision makers across the organization. Nowhere is this more evident than with the head honcho. It doesn't matter if you're an independent contractor or a twenty-year veteran of the company—at some point, you will have to get approval on *something* from *someone*. Wouldn't it be nice if you could walk into that meeting reasonably confident you'll walk out with a "yes"?

Of course it would. Here are some tips:

- **Befriend the admin assistants:** Administrative assistants often have a direct line to decision makers and understand their schedules, preferences, and expectations. Building

185

a relationship with them can smooth the way for scheduling meetings, understanding priorities, and even gathering insights into what might make your proposal more appealing.

- **Give them what they want:** Identify the key decision makers who have the power to approve or reject your budget or initiatives. Understand what they expect from marketing, whether through briefs, meetings, or other sources. Tailor your strategies to align with their goals and show how your proposals can meet their specific needs.

- **Presell everything:** The practice of marketing doesn't just apply to customers; it also applies to internal stakeholders. By presenting and discussing your strategies, creative ideas, and budgets with individual decision makers ahead of time (as much as is practical and allowable), you can walk into a presentation already confident that they will be receptive to your ideas. Preselling helps to create a room filled with allies rather than skeptics, paving the way for a successful outcome.

III. SALES AND BUSINESS DEVELOPMENT

The synergy between sales and the marketing teams is not just beneficial but also essential. This alignment goes beyond simple collaboration; it's a relationship where each team should work seamlessly with the other, driving the company forward. Sales and business development are marketing's closest allies, often acting as the practical application of marketing strategies and supporter of your voice of customer research.

By maintaining open communication, setting shared goals, and demonstrating mutual respect, sales and marketing collectively fuel an organization's growth engine. Recognize the value in each other's roles, honor commitments, and align your targets. This close-knit collaboration will not only make your daily operations smoother but also contribute significantly to achieving the organization's strategic objectives.

IV. ACCOUNTING, IT, AND OTHER DEPARTMENTS

It is all too easy for the accounting department to not pay a specific vendor, or for your latest website-related IT ticket to go unnoticed. From IT to accounting, you are going to need friends in all sorts of places. Don't overlook these teams; befriending them can (and will) save your hide and make your life generally more pleasant. Get your reports in on time, make reasonable technology requests, and don't demand that the shipping department do something "off the books." In general, be nice and be humble. It will pay dividends.

SO YOU WANT TO BE A SCIENCE MARKETER

A career in science marketing requires a unique blend of skills and interests. At the heart of this profession lies an insatiable curiosity and a general passion for understanding how things work. If you're considering transitioning from the laboratory into marketing—or even a *nonscientific* background into science marketing—here's what you need to know.

First and foremost, a successful science marketer possesses a can-do attitude. They're adept at fixing problems and controlling risks. An innate interest in the subject matter is vital, as developing marketing strategies and content requires true investment in the field. To create resonant messages, it helps to immerse oneself in

> AT THE HEART OF THIS PROFESSION LIES AN INSATIABLE CURIOSITY AND A GENERAL PASSION FOR UNDERSTANDING HOW THINGS WORK.

the scientific community by attending conferences, reading relevant publications, and genuinely finding the subject matter engaging. If you work for a science marketing agency, maintaining a broad interest in various scientific domains is beneficial, as clients may hail from diverse sectors.

In addition to curiosity and a problem-solving mindset, combining these core attributes with specialized skills can propel your career forward. Whether it's graphic design, copywriting and editing, development, event management, or media relations, having training and experience in an additional skill set can make you a multifaceted asset in science marketing.

Career paths in science marketing are as diverse as the sciences themselves. You may find opportunities with the internal marketing team at pharmaceutical companies, research institutions, and technology firms or within external marketing agencies with a focus on science and engineering organizations. Depending on your interests and skills, roles may range from content creation and brand management to event coordination and public relations.

WHAT THE WORLD NEEDS NOW (IS SCIENCE MARKETING)

At the distinct risk of sounding self-serving, the importance of science marketing today can't be overstated. In an era where humanity faces unprecedented challenges such as climate change, resource scarcity, energy deficits, food security, and global health threats, the role of science marketing stands at a critical juncture.

In my introductory chapter, I pitched the not-so-novel idea that some of the world's massive challenges might find solutions in scientific innovation. The urgency to bridge the gap between scientific discoveries and real-world applications has never been more potent. And it's here that the distinction between science *communication* and science *marketing* becomes important.

Science communication, as essential as it is, primarily serves an educational purpose. It translates the enigmatic language of specialists into generally accessible terms. Ideally, science communication fosters understanding and appreciation. It invites dialogue and engagement, paving the way for a scientifically literate society capable of critically evaluating information. It's how many scientists are trained to communicate—objectively. However, it often stops at the threshold of action.

WHILE SCIENCE COMMUNICATION EDUCATES AND ENLIGHTENS, SCIENCE MARKETING PERSUADES AND PROPELS.

Science marketing, in contrast, goes a step further. It's a strategic, persuasion-driven approach that targets specific audiences, resonating with their needs and desires. It's not merely about explaining science but about convincing, compelling, and converting knowledge into action. Whether it's adopting new technology, purchasing a revolutionary product, or rallying behind a life-altering cause, science marketing merges science with storytelling, emotion, and social relevance.

While science communication educates and enlightens, science marketing persuades and propels. One lays the foundation, and the other builds upon it. It guides decisions and ignites change. They operate in synergy—neither is superior, but their roles are distinct and complementary.

In the face of current global challenges, education alone falls short. The world needs more than just an understanding of the underlying science; it requires motivation to align actions with sustainable practices and innovative solutions. It calls for a blend of academia, industry, and government to collaborate in translating awareness into tangible steps. This collaborative effort fuels the engine that can steer humanity toward a sustainable path.

Science marketing, therefore, should play an increasingly important role as we work together to address these challenges. By harnessing the power of persuasion, it can galvanize individuals, communities, and even nations to align behaviors and policies with scientifically backed solutions. Marketing amplifies the voice of science, enabling it to resonate in places that matter most—from board room to policy chambers to kitchen tables.

AND NOW THE END (BUT NOT *THE* END)

We've covered a lot of terrain. Hopefully, you've recognized that marketing for science products and innovations is not simply a business pursuit; it can also be a vehicle for societal transformation. It's about more than selling a product; it's often about shaping perceptions, influencing behaviors, and driving progress. It's about taking science from the abstract to the real, all the way from the lab to our daily lives.

I hope that the science marketing path ahead of you winds enticingly with both promise and responsibility. The challenges you face may be significant, but the solutions lie within your grasp. It's your task now to extend that reach, to transform awareness into action, understanding into implementation. In a landscape of change in which technology and science stand at the forefront, we are the navigators.

May your own path in science marketing be filled with discovery, innovation, and profound impact. Your next step awaits. Here's to seizing it with passion and purpose.

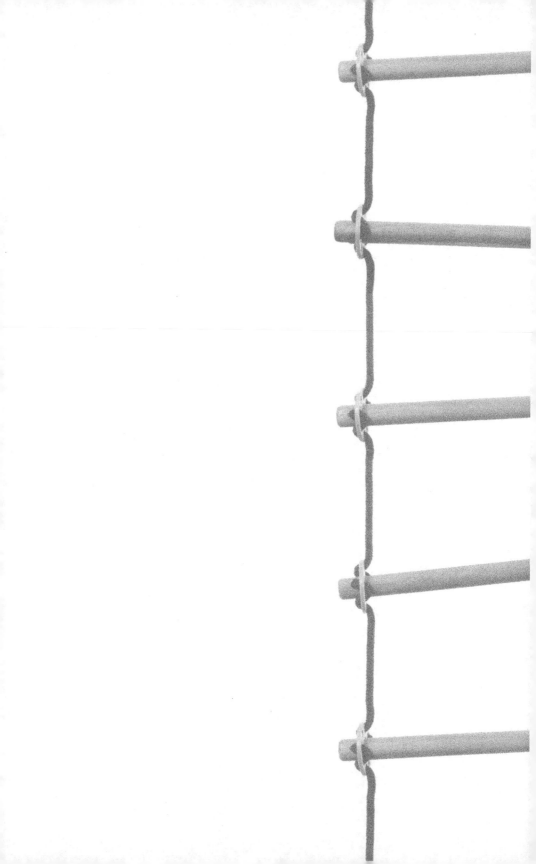